JOHN STUART MILL

AND REPRESENTATIVE GOVERNMENT

JOHN STUART MILL

AND REPRESENTATIVE

GOVERNMENT

Dennis F. Thompson

PRINCETON UNIVERSITY PRESS

Tried. 6.95 / 6.25 / 8 / 21 / 21

LCC 76-3023
ISBN 0-691-02187-2 (paperback edition)
ISBN 0-691-07582-4 (hardcover edition)

Publication of this book has been aided by a grant from
The Andrew W. Mellon Foundation

PRINTED IN THE UNITED STATES OF AMERICA
by Princeton University Press, Princeton, New Jersey

First PRINCETON PAPERBACK printing, 1979

Contents

Acknowledgments

I have benefited from the counsel of many persons in the writing of this book. Without abdicating responsibility for what appears in these pages, I wish to record my gratitude especially to Charles Beitz, Stanley Kelley, Jr., Richard Krouse, John Robson, Alan Ryan, Judith Shklar, Sanford Thatcher, and Edward Tufte. June Traube ably assisted with the preparation of the index.

I wrote the largest part of the manuscript while a Research Associate in Government at Harvard University during 1973-74. I am grateful to the Master and the members of Leverett House for helping to make that year pleasant and stimulating. Princeton University provided financial support for my leave and for the preparation of the manuscript for publication. My admiration for England and English thought deepened during two years at Oxford; for that experience, I am indebted to the U. S. Educational Commission in the United Kingdom and to the Master and Fellows of Balliol College.

JOHN STUART MILL

AND REPRESENTATIVE GOVERNMENT

Introduction

This study examines John Stuart Mill's theory of democracy as presented chiefly in *Considerations on Representative Government*, a work often neglected by commentators but considered by Mill to embody his "matured views" on "the best form of a popular constitution."[1] My principal aim is to explore the structure of Mill's theory, indicating how it combines the values of participation and competence, and showing that it is more coherent and systematic than has generally been assumed. Mill does not present a theory completely free of internal tensions, but most of those that remain are a deliberate consequence of his goal of formulating a comprehensive, balanced theory that leaves many conflicts to be resolved in practice in particular historical circumstances.

Observing that "democracy is too recent a phenomenon, of too great magnitude, for any one who now lives to comprehend its consequences," Mill suggested that any theory of democracy put forward in his time would have to be reconsidered by a "succession of thinkers and accurate observers" in light of "future experience."[2] In

[1] J. S. Mill, *Autobiography*, in *Autobiography and Other Writings*, ed. Jack Stillinger, Boston, 1969, p. 157.
[2] "M. de Tocqueville on Democracy in America," in *Dissertations and Discussions* (hereafter cited as "Tocqueville," in *DD*), New York, 1874, vol. II, pp. 113, 139.

the spirit of Mill's suggestion, my inquiry has a second purpose: to assess aspects of Mill's theory from the perspective of recent work in social science and democratic theory. The relationships between these studies and Mill's theory are complex, not only because Mill wrote more than a century earlier but also because Mill does not accept the now prevalent dichotomy between normative and empirical theory. But in some respects Mill's general approach to democracy can be seen as anticipating recent work and, more significantly, in other respects can be viewed as criticizing it.

Readers should not expect a chapter-by-chapter commentary on *Representative Government.* To reveal the structure of his theory more clearly, I give considerably greater emphasis to certain sections of the book than to others, and in some places alter the order of presentation of his arguments. Moreover, other writings, particularly the reviews of Tocqueville, *Utilitarianism,* and the *Logic,* will be invoked to clarify or elaborate ideas expressed in *Representative Government.* But generally I take Mill at his word and consider *Representative Government* as a work that stands on its own.

Despite the objections of some interpreters, we need not be reluctant to call Mill's theory a theory of democracy.[3] To do so is not misleading so long as we remember that the kind of democracy Mill favors gives a greater role to competence than do pure forms of democracy, and so long as we do not permit the label to substitute for a detailed analysis of the various compo-

[3] J. H. Burns, "J. S. Mill and Democracy, 1829-61," *Political Studies* 5 (June 1957), pp. 174-75; cf. Graeme Duncan, *Marx and Mill,* Cambridge, 1973, pp. 210-11, 258-59, 262, 264. But see Alan Ryan, "Two Concepts of Politics and Democracy: James and John Stuart Mill," in Martin Fleisher (ed.), *Machiavelli and the Nature of Political Thought,* New York, 1972, p. 100.

nents of the theory. Mill himself used "representative democracy" interchangeably with "representative government," and he did not hesitate to describe himself as a democrat in the middle as well as the later periods of his life.[4] His definition of representative government includes the basic characteristics of democracy: "sovereignty . . . vested in the entire aggregate of the community," a voice for every citizen in the exercise of that sovereignty, and participation by every citizen in the "discharge of some public function."[5] Mill, to be sure, circumscribes the exercise of this sovereignty in various ways, but most of the limitations are no greater, and in some respects less, than those imposed by other theorists who are generally regarded as democrats. Mill does not qualify in modern terms as a full-fledged participatory democrat, but neither can he be considered an elitist democrat. The complex nature of his theory cannot be captured by a label, but must be shown by a full analysis of its structure.

Among Mill's major writings on society and politics, *Representative Government* has enjoyed the least reputation as a serious contribution to social or political theory. In a generally sympathetic survey of utilitarian thought, Leslie Stephen in 1900 classed the book with the speeches of statesmen, which, though they may contain a "good deal of wisdom," are so inextricably mixed with "personal and practical remarks" that they cannot be regarded as systematic political theory.[6] Later com-

[4] *Considerations on Representative Government* (hereafter cited as *CRG*), 3d ed., London, 1865, ch. VIII, pp. 131, 163-64; ch. V, pp. 87-88; ch. VI, pp. 110, 117; ch. XIII, p. 242; and *Autobiography*, ch. V, pp. 102-3; ch. VII, pp. 137-38.

[5] *CRG*, ch. III, p. 53.

[6] Leslie Stephen, *The English Utilitarians*, London, 1900, vol. III, pp. 273-74.

mentators have pronounced only slightly less harsh judgments upon the book and have usually accorded it little
more attention than Stephen did.[7]

When recent scholars *have* examined Mill's thought
on representative government, they have most often
viewed it historically, showing how his later ideas
evolved from his earlier writings and how the various
strains in his thinking arose from influences on him at
different periods during his life.[8] *Representative Government* appears only incidentally in these interpretations, usually to illustrate ideas Mill expressed earlier.
Mill gives some warrant for this approach, prefacing
Representative Government with the admonition that
readers of his previous work will receive "no strong impression of novelty from the present volume; for the
principles are those to which I have been working up
during the greater part of my life." But he immediately
goes on to claim that "there is novelty . . . in the fact
of bringing them together, and exhibiting them in their
connexion; and . . . in much that is brought forward in
their support."[9] The *Autobiography* reaffirms his view

[7] Cf. A. D. Lindsay, "Introduction," in *Utilitarianism, Liberty
and Representative Government*, New York, 1951, p. xxviii; and
Noel Annan, "John Stuart Mill," in Hugh S. Davies and George
Watson (eds.), *The English Mind*, Cambridge, Eng., 1964, p. 228.
John Plamenatz allows that *Representative Government* is "full of
good arguments," but he barely discusses them at all (*The
English Utilitarians*, 2d ed., Oxford, 1958, p. 134). Robert Cumming disregards Mill's writings on representative government in
part because they have been "less influential on later political
thought" (*Human Nature and History*, Chicago, 1969, vol. 1,
p. 48).

[8] Joseph Hamburger, *Intellectuals in Politics*, New Haven,
1965; R. P. Anschutz, *The Philosophy of J. S. Mill*, Oxford, 1963,
pp. 30-60; and Burns, *Political Studies* 5 (June and Oct. 1957), pp.
158-75, 281-94.

[9] *CRG*, Preface, p. v.

that *Representative Government* presents a "connected exposition" of his democratic theory.[10]

Partly because commentators do not consider the theory in *Representative Government* as a "connected exposition" on its own terms, they tend to present an account of the theory that is, at best, partial. The most common reading of the theory, at least among Mill scholars, emphasizes its elitist elements, especially rule by the "instructed few." "Mill's purpose . . . in everything . . . written after his crisis," Shirley Letwin asserts, "was exactly contrary to Bentham's. He meant to secure the leadership of those who knew better."[11] This aspect of Mill's thought so dominates these interpretations that its democratic elements almost vanish from view. Indeed, J. H. Burns concludes that a "consistent viewpoint unites Mill's political thought from start to finish; but

[10] *Autobiography*, ch. VII, p. 157.

[11] Shirley Letwin, *The Pursuit of Certainty*, Cambridge, Eng., 1965, p. 306. A few pages later (p. 310) she recognizes that Mill tries to combine "broad political participation with leadership by those who know best," but asserts that his effort fails. Gertrude Himmelfarb treats *Representative Government*, which she mentions only in a footnote, as belonging to the "corpus of the 'other' Mill," who emphasizes elitist ideas more than does the Mill of *On Liberty*, on which her study concentrates (*On Liberty and Liberalism*, New York, 1974, pp. 303-4n). Willmoore Kendall and George Carey, while claiming that to "put Mill down as an elitist *tout court* . . . is . . . an oversimplification," write that *Representative Government* is "an early expression of the state of mind, the mind-set, which permeates contemporary elitist thinking. . ." ("The 'Roster Device': J. S. Mill and Contemporary Elitism," *Western Political Quarterly* 21 [March 1968], p. 38). According to Bruce Mazlish, Mill, an "elitist of sorts," had "one constant motive" in advocating the institutions described in *Representative Government*: "to block the tyranny of the majority, and to ensure that the 'interests' of the cultivated individual, society and humanity would be honored" (*James and John Stuart Mill*, New York, 1975, p. 401).

7

it is not, in the strict sense he would have adopted, the viewpoint of a democrat."[12] At the other extreme, Mill has often been cited as an exponent of classical democratic theory; this view enunciates only his commitment to participation.[13] Some interpreters emphasize both the elitist and participatory strains in Mill's thought, but they usually end up charging him with inconsistency. R. P. Anschutz, for example, argues that by the time Mill wrote *Representative Government* his "political thinking [had] developed along two quite different and inconsistent lines." He had become more of a democrat, urging more democracy as a cure for the ills of democracy, and also less of a democrat, decrying the "tendency of democracy towards bearing down individuality and circumscribing the exercise of human faculties."[14] Presenting a more subtle and comprehensive account of Mill's effort to combine democratic and elitist ideas, Graeme Duncan nevertheless finds the result to be an "untidy and unsuccessful compromise."[15]

[12] Burns, pp. 174-75. Mill does not consider himself a majority-rule democrat, but this is not the only sense, or even the strict sense, in which he uses "democracy." See note 4, above.

[13] Graeme Duncan and Steven Lukes, "The New Democracy," *Political Studies* 11 (June 1963), pp. 158-60; Jack L. Walker, "A Critique of the Elitist Theory of Democracy," *American Political Science Review* 60 (June 1966), p. 288; and Peter Bachrach, *The Theory of Democratic Elitism*, Boston, 1967, pp. 3-5. Duncan later concedes that "The New Democracy" gave too much weight to the participatory elements in Mill's thought ("John Stuart Mill and Democracy," *Politics* 4 [May 1969], p. 80n).

[14] Anschutz, p. 32. Also see Carole Pateman, *Participation and Democratic Theory*, Cambridge, Eng., 1970, p. 28; and Lindsay, pp. xxviii-xxix.

[15] Duncan, *Marx and Mill*, esp. p. 259. John M. Robson presents a carefully balanced interpretation, but makes no attempt to analyze the structure of the theory in *CRG* or its contemporary validity (*The Improvement of Mankind*, Toronto, 1968, pp. 222-

Contrary to most interpretations, this study treats *Representative Government* as a "connected exposition" of a democratic theory that, with some success, combines the values of both participation and competence. Mill sets forth two very general criteria for the "goodness of a government": the degree to which "it is adapted to take advantage of the amount of good qualities" in the governed that exist at any particular time; and the degree to which "it tends to increase the sum of good qualities in the governed." The first criterion refers to what may be called the protective goal, since Mill would consider it satisfied to the extent that the interests of citizens and the general interest are protected in the institutions of government. The second criterion (for Mill the more important one) refers to what may be termed the educative goal, because it deals with government as an "agency of national education."[16]

Applying these criteria, Mill in effect invokes two principles. The first, which will be called the principle of participation, requires that the participation of each citizen be as great as possible to promote both the protective and the educative goals of government. Mill's arguments for extensive participation appeal to the need to protect the interests of each citizen and to improve the political intelligence of all citizens. The second, which will be termed the principle of competence, stipulates that the influence of the more qualified citizens should be as great as possible to promote both the pro-

---

44). Ryan also clearly recognizes the complexity and range of the values Mill expresses in *CRG*, as well as the contemporary significance of the book, though he does not examine its theoretical structure in any detail (*J. S. Mill*, London, 1974, pp. 190-217).

[16] *CRG*, ch. II, pp. 30-34. The terms are suggested by Pateman, pp. 19-21.

9

tective and the educative goals. Here Mill appeals to the need for competent leadership to protect against the dangers of ignorance and of sinister interests in the government and among the public, and to contribute to the process of civic education.

Although the two principles set the same goals, they call for different means to realize those goals and, therefore, often conflict with each other. Even in Chapter III of *Representative Government*, almost exclusively a defense of participation, the principle of competence intrudes. Mill concludes that participation should be as great as "the general degree of improvement of the community will allow," implying that a society must reach a certain level of competence before the principle of participation operates at all.[17] The principle of competence also constrains the principle of participation in more advanced societies, where this level is reached; even here ". . . the wiser or better man, has a claim to superior weight."[18] But such qualifications do not nullify the claim of the principle of participation; they do not, as some writers suggest, carry Mill's "whole meaning."[19] Indeed, if extensive participation promotes civic education, Mill is willing to forgive "almost any amount of other demerit" in a system of government, such as, presumably, a certain amount of incompetence.[20] The principle of participation constrains the principle of competence, just as the latter principle limits the former. Mill's aim is to "secure, as far as they can be made compatible," the advantage of government by the competent along with the advantage of government made

[17] *CRG*, ch. III, p. 69.   [18] *CRG*, ch. VIII, p. 174.
[19] E.g., George Sabine, *A History of Political Theory*, 3d ed., New York, 1961, p. 707.
[20] *CRG*, ch. II, p. 36.

responsible through participation by citizens. Thus, the two principles evidently are "coequal."[21]

The problem for Mill, then, becomes how to reconcile the two principles. A synthesis of the principles takes place in practical political life in two general ways. First, a balance between the values of participation and competence may be achieved *at any particular time* through political institutions or processes that are designed to realize both values simultaneously. A theory of government characterizes the nature of these institutions and the standards by which they may be evaluated. Second, the tension between participation and competence is reduced *over time* by the gradual improvement of the competence of all citizens through participation. A theory of development locates this improvement within a general process of historical evolution.

To understand how Mill proposes to combine the two principles, we first need to examine each one separately; then we can consider his efforts to join them in the theory of government and the theory of development. The concluding chapter identifies some of the major deficiencies in Mill's theory and suggests some ways in which the theory could be modified to overcome them.

[21] *CRG*, ch. VI, pp. 116-17; ch. XII, p. 227.

1

The Principle of Participation

Mill's enthusiasm for participation pervades the third chapter of *Representative Government*, where he seeks to show "that the only government which can fully satisfy all the exigencies of the social state, is one in which the whole people participate; [and] that any participation, even in the smallest public function, is useful."[1] Mill so warms to the subject that the chapter approaches a vindication of direct democracy; not until the last sentence, which intrudes almost as an afterthought, does Mill dismiss that kind of democracy (because it is impracticable except in small towns). Mill of course resists direct democracy for another reason, too (elaborated in other chapters of *Representative Government*): only a representative government can give sufficient influence to persons of superior competence. Even so, Mill's representative government offers citizens more scope for political participation than do the systems advocated by many modern democratic theorists, and in some respects even more than do those of theorists, such as Rousseau, who are often counted as radical democrats. Mill's participatory ardor springs from his beliefs that extensive participation promotes, first, the "present well-being" of society by protecting the interests of citizens and, second, a "better and higher form of na-

[1] *CRG*, ch. III, p. 69.

tional character" by facilitating the political education of citizens.[2] These beliefs, respectively, are the core of his protective and educative arguments for the principle of participation.

THE PROTECTIVE ARGUMENT

The first proposition on which the protective argument for participation rests is that

> the rights and interests of every or any person are only secure from being disregarded, when the person interested is himself able, and habitually disposed, to stand up for them. . . . [Alternatively,] each is the only safe guardian of his own rights and interests.[3]

Two different assumptions support these propositions, one relating to motivation and the other to the knowledge on which individuals act. The motivational assumption holds that "mankind, as a rule, prefer themselves to others, and those nearest to them to those more remote."[4] Earlier Mill had criticized Bentham and other utilitarians for founding a whole ethical theory on such

[2] CRG, ch. III, pp. 54, 58.
[3] CRG, ch. III, pp. 54, 55. The idea of a right disappears in Mill's defense of the proposition. Presumably, because both right and interests are defined in terms of utility, Mill feels that he need directly discuss only one of the two ideas; in any case, in his later discussion of the right to vote (see Chapter 3, below) Mill actually rejects any independent justification of participation based on rights. See *Utilitarianism*, in *Collected Works of John Stuart Mill* (hereafter cited as *CW*), ed. John M. Robson, Toronto, 1969, vol. x, ch. v, p. 250.
[4] CRG, ch. III, p. 55. Although Mill initially treats this assumption as inessential to his argument, he nevertheless appeals to it at a number of crucial points.

an assumption, and he has not changed his mind about that.[5] But he now seeks to support a theory of government under conditions where men cannot be expected to live up to the stringent demands of a general theory of ethics. His analysis of the "Benthamic theory" in the *Logic* indicates how he intends to limit the scope of the motivational assumption. When the Benthamites contended that "men's actions are determined by their interests," they sometimes wrote as if interest meant "anything a person likes."[6] But from this concept of interest, Mill notes, they could not draw the implications they wished; presumably, he means that any proposition using such a broad concept of interest would be vacuous.[7]

[5] "Remarks on Bentham's Philosophy," in *CW*, vol. x, pp. 13-16; "Bentham," in *CW*, vol. x, pp. 94-99; and *Utilitarianism*, ch. II, pp. 214-22.

[6] *A System of Logic*, in *CW*, Toronto, 1974, vol. VIII, Bk. VI, ch. viii, § 3, p. 890. Some recent commentators also take this as the Benthamites' intention. See, e.g., A. J. Ayer, "The Principle of Utility," in *Philosophical Essays*, London, 1954, pp. 253-54; and Hanna Pitkin, *The Concept of Representation*, Berkeley and Los Angeles, 1967, pp. 204-5.

[7] Mill himself occasionally uses an equally broad and subjective concept of interest: "A man's interest consists of whatever he takes an interest in" (*CRG*, ch. x, pp. 210-12; also ch. VI, pp. 123-24). But usually Mill is careful to distinguish various kinds of interests. For example, apparent interests refer to those objects of desire which an individual believes will satisfy him, whereas real interests are those which would actually do so in the long run (ch. VI, pp. 121-23). Then there is the general interest, an "impartial regard for the interest of all" including the "permanent interests of man as a progressive being"; it is contrasted with particular or selfish interests and with sinister interests, those which conflict "more or less with the general good of the community" (ch. VI, pp. 118, 121-23; *On Liberty*, London, 1854, ch. I, p. 24). Generally on the concept of interest in utilitarianism, see Brian Barry, *Political Argument*, London, 1965, pp. 173-86; Richard E. Flathman, *The Public Interest*, New York, 1966, esp. pp. 14-31; and Pitkin, pp. 156-62.

Mill thinks that the Benthamites intended to say that men's actions are determined by their "selfish" (or "private or worldly") interests. Although, according to Mill, this assertion is not universally true (and therefore cannot be the foundation of a general theory of motivation or ethics), it is generally true of large groups of men under present social conditions (and hence is a sensible assumption on which to base a practical political theory).

Mill follows Hume here: "It is, therefore, a just *political* maxim, *that every man must be supposed a knave*; though . . . it appears strange that a maxim should be true in *politics* which is false *in fact*."[8] The social psychology behind Hume's dictum is very similar to Mill's. According to Hume, the social habits that make men care for others' interests as much as their own develop in close personal relations and spontaneously operate only in the family, among friends, and in small groups. As men learn the advantages of cooperation, as they adopt social rules and establish governments, artificial institutions curb somewhat this natural partiality toward themselves and their close associates. But it remains a potent force, especially in political life, which exhibits few of the features of close personal relations; to the extent politics does have these features, loyalty toward one's group or faction prevails against the general interest. Politics can thus bring out the worst in men.[9] Similarly, Mill believes that we cannot safely expect political men to pursue more than their self-inter-

[8] David Hume, "Of the Independency of Parliament," in *Essays*, Oxford, 1963, p. 42. James Mill quotes Hume's dictum in *Fragment on Mackintosh*, London, 1870, p. 278.

[9] "Independency," p. 43; and *A Treatise of Human Nature*, ed. L. A. Selby-Bigge, Oxford, 1960, Bk. III, Pt. II, pp. 484-89, 534-35; Pt. III, pp. 583-84, 602-3.

ests. A more extended sense of sympathy or concern for the general interest requires a greater appreciation of the more remote consequences of actions and a more highly developed imagination; at present these qualities are found only among the better educated members of society.[10] The potential effect of education gives Mill some reason to hope that these dismal propensities in political life may be subdued in the future, but in the meantime

> Governments must be made for human beings as they are, or as they are capable of speedily becoming. . . . And it cannot be maintained that any form of government would be rational, which required as a condition that these exalted principles [such as "a disinterested regard for others"] . . . should be the guiding and master motives in the conduct of average human beings.[11]

The immediate object of these remarks is the democratic majority, but Mill plainly thinks that any ruling group must be assumed to suffer from the same infirmities.[12]

Unless we can say that minorities are more likely to pursue selfish interests than the democratic majority, the motivational assumption alone cannot establish that maximum participation would be better than minority rule. If everyone must be assumed to pursue selfish interests, no group would have any more title than any other to rule in the general interest. We cannot decide *a priori* who is more inclined to pursue selfish interests —the rulers or the people. Mill is sensitive to this point

[10] *CRG*, ch. VI, pp. 125-26; ch. III, pp. 55-56.
[11] *CRG*, ch. VI, pp. 125-26.
[12] *CRG*, ch. VI, pp. 121-22.

because his father ignored it, thereby falling victim to a cogent rebuke from Macaulay.[13] Mill thinks that both rulers and citizens are likely to pursue sinister interests when they have unrestrained power, and government must protect against both possibilities.[14] He therefore needs an argument that does not depend on the false claim that rulers are always more inclined to pursue sinister or selfish interests than citizens are. Hence, he argues from the supposition that is least favorable to the case for democratic participation: even if rulers are benevolent, genuinely seeking to act in the interests of their subjects, they cannot reliably or fully know what these interests are unless citizens themselves have a chance to express them.

> We need not suppose that when power resides in an exclusive class, that class will knowingly and deliberately sacrifice the other classes to themselves: it suffices that, in the absence of its natural defenders, the interest of the excluded is always in danger of being overlooked; and, when looked at, is seen with very different eyes from those of the persons whom it directly concerns.[15]

Carried to an extreme, this view would deny the possibility of representation altogether, as Rousseau does in the *Social Contract*.[16] Mill of course does not go so far; he applies the idea only to classes or groups of in-

---

[13] T. B. Macaulay, "Mill on Government," in *Miscellaneous Writings of Lord Macaulay*, London, 1860, vol. I, pp. 288-95. Cf. Mill, *Autobiography*, ch v, pp. 95-97.

[14] *Logic*, Bk. VI, ch. viii, § 3, pp. 889-94; and *CRG*, ch. VI, pp. 125-27.

[15] *CRG*, ch. III, p. 56.

[16] *Du contrat social*, in *The Political Writings of Jean-Jacques Rousseau*, ed. C. E. Vaughan, Oxford, 1962, vol. II, Bk. II, ch. 1.

dividuals, such as women and the working class. In this respect, however, he goes beyond his father, who thought that women's interests would be adequately represented by their husbands, and that men over forty would look after the interests of youth.[17]

Mill is not saying that individuals or groups always know their own interests best.[18] Although he subscribes to something like this view in *On Liberty*, he does not extend it to other-regarding activities, with which society and government are properly concerned.[19] Even within the self-regarding sphere, Mill presses only the negative point that government and society usually do not know better than an individual what is in his interest, though he might not know very well either. Mill's defense of laissez-faire in *Political Economy* appeals to the principle that "most persons take a juster and more intelligent view of their own interest, and of the means of promoting it, than can either be prescribed to them by a general enactment of the legislature, or pointed out in the particular case by a public functionary."[20] But by the time Mill finishes listing the "large and conspicuous exceptions" to this principle, its scope has contracted drastically. For his argument in *Representative Government* Mill needs only the cautious claim that a group or class sometimes perceives its interests better than others do, and that the interests of any group excluded from the political process are therefore not likely to be accurately or fully represented by others.

[17] James Mill, *An Essay on Government*, Indianapolis, 1955, ch. VIII, pp. 73-75. Cf. *CRG*, ch. VIII, pp. 184-88; and J. S. Mill, *The Subjection of Women*, London, 1869, ch. III, pp. 95-97.

[18] Anschutz (p. 57) seems to ascribe such a view to Mill.

[19] *Liberty*, ch. IV, pp. 135-38, 149-51.

[20] *Principles of Political Economy*, in *CW*, vol. III, Toronto, 1965, Bk. V, ch. xi, § 9, pp. 951 ff.

Some commentators suggest that Mill implicitly adopts the familiar "shoes-pinching" argument here to justify the principle of participation.[21] Citizens at least know when the results of governmental decisions and laws affect them adversely, and since the aim of government generally cannot be to affect citizens adversely, the opinions of citizens about the effects of government must have some validity. The argument has a long and distinguished history—Aristotle used it and twentieth-century theorists still appeal to it[22]—but fortunately Mill does not rely on it solely since, for two reasons, it cannot alone justify the principle of participation. First, benevolent rulers can discover the opinions of citizens through means other than participation—for example, by public opinion polls. If we add, as some theorists do, the further premise that rulers will not be likely to heed the opinions of citizens unless the opinions are backed by the sanction of elections, we undermine the supposition of benevolent rule, on which Mill wishes to ground his reasoning at this stage. Second, the most that the shoes-pinching argument could justify would be voting on policies after they had been implemented and on candidates after they had made political decisions that affected citizens. Although some political scientists interpret electoral decisions in much this way—as a broad verdict on past performance[23]—Mill

[21] Pitkin, pp. 204-5.

[22] Aristotle, *Politics*, tr. H. Rackham, Cambridge, Mass., 1967, Bk. III, 1281.b39 – 1282.b24, pp. 224-27; A. D. Lindsay, *The Modern Democratic State*, New York, 1962, pp. 269-71; Charles Merriam, *The New Democracy and The New Despotism*, New York, 1939, p. 41; and Harold J. Laski, *The Limitations of the Expert*, London, 1931, pp. 12-13.

[23] V. O. Key, *Public Opinion and American Democracy*, New York, 1961, p. 473; and Angus Campbell et al., *The American Voter*, New York, 1960, pp. 525-27.

insists that opinions or apparent interests of citizens and their representatives should play a greater role than this in the political process. The opinions of the working class on the question of strikes, for example, ought to be expressed in Parliament by members of the working class.[24]

Mill's conception of the role of ordinary citizens' opinions in elections has also been compared to Joseph Schumpeter's view that citizens should decide only which candidates are chosen among competing elites, not what policies are adopted.[25] Mill does seem to take a very similar stance in an earlier essay: the judgment of "the many . . . must in general be exercised rather upon the characters and talents of the persons whom they appoint to decide [political] questions for them than upon the questions themselves."[26] But *Representative Government* expands the political role of ordinary citizens. Even though Mill still hopes that citizens will choose the wisest person to represent them, he now maintains that it is inevitable and even desirable that citizens' opinions about their own interests and about substantive political issues influence their choice of representatives.[27] It is not that Mill trusts citizens' opinions more than Schumpeter, but rather that Mill expects to see some improvement in the quality of those opinions through the educative effects of participation, while Schumpeter and many of his followers among contemporary political scientists do not.

[24] *CRG*, ch. III, pp. 56-57.

[25] Hamburger, p. 89n. See Joseph Schumpeter, *Capitalism, Socialism and Democracy*, 3d ed., New York, 1962, pp. 235-302.

[26] J. S. Mill, "The Rationale of Political Representation," *London Review* 1 (July 1835), pp. 348-49.

[27] *CRG*, ch. XII, pp. 230-31. See Chapter 3, below, pp. 114-15.

So far Mill has sought to show that the interests of nonparticipants are likely to be overlooked or misperceived. He still needs to establish that if nonparticipants become participants, their interests will be taken into account. Does participation in fact make a difference in the policies adopted by governments? This is an empirical question, and when Mill looks for evidence to answer it, he is handicapped by the scarcity of examples of democratic governments in his own time. He is forced to turn to historical comparisons of relatively free states (such as the Italian republics and the independent towns of Flanders, Germany, England, Switzerland and Holland) with relatively unfree states existing at the same time (such as the European feudal monarchies, Austria and prerevolutionary France). The former carried out more just policies and were more responsive to their citizens than were the latter.[28] Even if this evidence pertains to democracies, it is suspect for reasons that Mill himself gives in the *Logic*. There Mill purports to prove that his "method of difference," which seems to underlie the empirical argument for participation, does not work in social science. If we wished to show, for example, the effects of a restrictive and prohibitory commercial legislation upon national wealth, we would have to compare at least two countries "whose habits, usages, opinions, laws and institutions are the same in all respects, except that one of them has a more protective tariff. . . ."[29] Although it may be said that Mill's standard of proof here almost makes social science impossible and that Mill himself does not observe it,[30]

[28] *CRG*, ch. III, pp. 57-58.
[29] *Logic*, Bk. VI, ch. vii, § 3, pp. 883-84.
[30] See Alan Ryan, *John Stuart Mill*, New York, 1970, pp. 137-40.

nevertheless he does not in *Representative Government* adequately come to grips with the difficulties that his standard raises. He does not try to rule out other effects, such as political culture or class structure, that could account for the differences in governmental policies as much as could the relative freedom created by the political institutions.

Modern empirical studies that bear on Mill's argument give somewhat better support to it than he himself supplied. Two consequences of more extensive participation offer some indirect support. First, the social composition of political leadership has shifted somewhat toward social classes that were excluded in Mill's time (though even in the Labour party in Britain the middle classes have been more predominantly represented among M.P.s and leaders than have the working classes, and working-class representation in Labour cabinets reached its high point in 1924).[31] Second, political competition has increased as participation has become more extensive. During Mill's time the proportion of contested parliamentary seats grew from 43 percent in 1835 to 77 percent in 1880.[32] If increased competition

[31] Richard Rose, "Class and Party Divisions: Britain as a Test Case," *Sociology* 2 (May 1968), pp. 129-62; W. L. Guttsman, "The British Political Elite and Class Structure," in Philip Stanworth and Anthony Giddens (eds.), *Elites and Power in British Society*, Cambridge, Eng., 1974, pp. 32-33; Ralf Dahrendorf, "Recent Changes in the Class Structure of European Societies," *Daedalus* 93 (Winter 1964), pp. 225-70; and Mattei Dogan, "Political Ascent in a Class Society: French Deputies, 1870-1958," in Dwaine Marvick (ed.), *Political Decision-Makers*, Glencoe, Ill., 1961, pp. 57-90.

[32] Data are from Norman Gash, *Politics in the Age of Peel*, London, 1953, p. 441; and Harold J. Hanham, *Elections and Party Management*, London, 1959, p. 197. Generally on the association between competitiveness and participation, see Stanley Kelley, Jr., Richard E. Ayres, and William G. Bowen, "Registra-

permits more interests to be expressed, then participation tends to enlarge the range of interests that can be taken into consideration, as Mill hoped.

More direct evidence about the effects of participation on governmental policies is harder to secure. Some studies of state government in the United States indicate that greater participation has an effect on certain kinds of policies adopted by the government; for example, as the level of participation goes up, the ratio of benefits to tax burdens for lower-income groups also tends to go up.[33] The best evidence now available is Verba and Nie's study of forty-two American communities, which concludes, *inter alia*, that participation makes some difference in the responsiveness of political leaders. The more citizens participate, the more likely leaders are to "adopt the same agenda for community action" as citizens would. This conclusion holds true at the individual level even when social and economic variables are held constant; citizens who participate more are more likely to have leaders agree with them. It also holds for a system as a whole; in systems that have relatively high levels of participation, leaders are more responsive to inactive as well as active citizens—and more responsive to the active citizens than to the inactive citizens.[34]

---

tion and Voting: Putting First Things First," *American Political Science Review* 61 (June 1967), pp. 365-66; and Walter Dean Burnham, "The Changing Shape of the American Political Universe," *American Political Science Review* 59 (March 1965), pp. 22-28.

[33] Brian R. Fry and Richard F. Winters, "The Politics of Redistribution," *American Political Science Review* 64 (June 1970), pp. 508-22 (and the citations there).

[34] Sidney Verba and Norman H. Nie, *Participation in America*, New York, 1972, pp. 332-33, 299-308, 306-7. Verba and Nie concede that their findings are consistent with the alternative hy-

If participation influences governmental decisions in this way, Mill has some basis for maintaining that individuals are the safest guardians of their own interests. The justification of the principle of participation is not yet complete, however, because the interests that individuals guard are not necessarily their real interests or the general interest. The well-being of all members of society (which should be understood to include the "permanent interests of man as a progressive being") is the sole object of government, and it cannot be achieved by merely adding up the particular interests of all citizens.[35] Unlike Bentham and James Mill,[36] the younger Mill repudiates the view that the general interest is simply the sum of all individual interests. How can the object of government be achieved then? Or to put the question another way: if the proposition that each is the safest guardian of his own interests is a maxim of prudence, as Mill maintains, how can he derive from it the principle of participation, which is a maxim of ethics?[37]

Faced with a similar problem in *Utilitarianism*, Mill suggests that individuals' interests may come to be more

---

pothesis that citizens are more responsive to leaders as participation increases, but the authors present some indirect evidence that casts doubts on this hypothesis (pp. 304, 331-32).

[35] *CRG*, ch. II, pp. 17-18, 30; *Liberty*, ch. I, p. 24.

[36] See Jeremy Bentham, *An Introduction to the Principles of Morals and Legislation*, ed. J. H. Burns and H.L.A. Hart, London, 1970, ch. I, pp. 11-13; *Plan of Parliamentary Reform*, in *The Works of Jeremy Bentham*, ed. John Bowring, Edinburgh, 1843, vol. III, pp. 445-51; *Leading Principles of a Constitutional Code*, in *Works*, vol. II, p. 269; and James Mill, *Essay on Government*, ch. VII, p. 69.

[37] *CRG*, ch. III, p. 55. For Mill's distinction among the "three departments" of the "Art of Life" (morality, prudence or policy, and aesthetics), see *Logic*, Bk. VI, ch. xii, § 7.

closely identified with the general interest through "the improvement of education." Until that happens, the interests of morally superior individuals count for more in arriving at the total utility.[38] He makes a similar move in *Representative Government*, but attempts to design institutions that will achieve this goal of competence without sacrificing democracy. I shall examine the adequacy of this solution later, but it should be already evident that the protective argument cannot alone establish the principle of participation. Mill recognizes that he cannot do without an educative argument for participation.

A second part of the protective argument remains to be considered:

> [T]he general prosperity attains a greater height, and is more widely diffused, in proportion to the amount and variety of the personal energies enlisted in promoting it.[39]

Since Mill does not elaborate on this proposition, its meaning is not entirely clear. The basic idea evidently is that in a popular government citizens are more likely to acquire the habit of doing things for themselves and that as a result the general level of prosperity—mainly economic—will be raised. The evidence he offers for the proposition is the same historical evidence that he cited to suggest that more interests are better protected in relatively free states. The evidence is vulnerable to the same objections we noted above, but again we can use some contemporary studies to bolster Mill's claim. That the levels of political and economic development of societies are highly correlated has been fairly well

[38] *Utilitarianism*, ch. III, pp. 231-32.
[39] *CRG*, ch. III, p. 54.

established. The more competitive a political regime and the more extensive the rights of participation, the more likely the country will be at a relatively high social and economic level (and vice versa).[40] Mill may have been impressed, from his reading of Tocqueville, that the main features of democratic politics had been established in the United States before the country had reached a high level of economic development.[41] Recent work suggests that Tocqueville's assessment of American economic development was in this respect correct.[42] But if Mill intended to assert that democratic participation is a necessary condition of economic development, or of a fairly high level of prosperity, his assertion would not be borne out by any evidence now available. There are today a number of examples of relatively undemocratic countries (such as the Soviet Union and East Germany) that stand higher on the scale of economic prosperity than do relatively more democratic countries (such as India until recently). Indeed, Prussia in Mill's own time would probably have qualified as an example of the former. The precise nature of the causal relation between economic prosperity and political democracy remains obscure, but it is surely not unidirectional. Probably Mill did not intend to offer a rigorous causal hy-

[40] Irma Adelman and Cynthia Taft Morris, *Society, Politics, and Economic Development*, Baltimore, 1967, esp. p. 262; Deane E. Neubauer, "Some Conditions of Democracy," *American Political Science Review* 61 (Dec. 1967), pp. 1002-9; and Bruce M. Russett, *Trends in World Politics*, New York, 1965, pp. 125-26. The best brief discussion of the evidence is in Robert A. Dahl, *Polyarchy*, New Haven, 1971, pp. 62-80. For further evidence and qualifications, see Robert W. Jackman, *Politics and Social Equality*, New York, 1975, pp. 84-85.

[41] Cf. Mill, "Tocqueville," in *DD*, pp. 103-4.

[42] See Ralph Andreano (ed.), *New Views on American Economic Development*, Cambridge, Mass., 1965.

pothesis on the subject. If he meant merely that political democracy and economic prosperity tend to go together, he would not have to alter his view today, except to admit that this part of his case for participation is not conclusive.

THE EDUCATIVE ARGUMENT AND NATIONAL CHARACTER

According to Mill's educative argument, which he regards as more important than the protective argument, participation fosters the development of a vigorous, public-spirited "national character."[43] This argument enables Mill to transcend the protective argument in two respects. First, he can urge more participation even where it would not be necessary to express interests. If participation educates citizens, the utility of increasing it is virtually unlimited. Even when he believes that more extensive political involvement would not make any difference in the policies of government, he still favors it for educational reasons.[44] Second, he can call for greater participation where it would not otherwise contribute to the general interest. If political activity helps educate citizens, then any present failure of citizens to act in the general interest or their real interest can be overcome by more participation. The pursuit of self-interest is so deeply rooted in human behavior because existing institutions encourage it; as these institutions are changed, civic education can eventually create an "interest in the common good." In the meantime, Mill's expectations are more modest. He would be satisfied with

[43] *CRG*, ch. III, pp. 58-69. On Mill's opinion of the significance of this argument, see ch. II, pp. 30, 34-35, 37; ch. xv, pp. 277-78.
[44] "Recent Writers on Reform," in *DD*, vol. IV, pp. 60-61.

something between selfishness and altruism— "enlightened self-interest."[45]

Although Bentham also believed that education is an essential part of a democratic society, he generally thought of education in terms of formal schooling. His *Chrestomathia* stressed the teaching of basic skills such as reading and vocational training of various kinds. A broader notion of education, encompassing the whole range of experiences that shape human character, never found its way into his political theory.[46] The younger Mill considered this to be one of Bentham's greatest shortcomings. Bentham does not attempt to portray one type of character as preferable to another because he takes "human beings as he finds them" and endeavors only "to supply such inducements that will constrain even persons of dispositions most at variance with the general happiness."[47]

The great advantage of Bentham's approach, which Mill does not mention, is that it escapes the burden of justifying the choice of one type of character over another. The orthodox utilitarians did not need to carry their argument beyond an appeal to the actual preferences of individuals, corrected only to make them socially compatible and individually satisfying as judged by the individuals themselves. But since Mill takes exception to

[45] *Autobiography*, ch. vii, pp. 138-39; and "Tocqueville," in *DD*, pp. 141-42.

[46] Bentham, *Chrestomathia*, in *Works*, vol. viii, pp. 1-191. James Mill explicitly takes a wider view of education, but he does not relate it to his theory of representative government ("Education," in *James Mill on Education*, ed. W. H. Burston, Cambridge, Eng., 1969, pp. 41-119).

[47] Mill, "Remarks . . . ," pp. 8-9; and "Bentham," pp. 94-96, 99. "Remarks" first appeared anonymously in an appendix to Lytton Bulwer's *England and the English*, London, 1833; in the later essay Mill softens his criticisms of Bentham.

the character of "human beings as he finds them," he must justify an ideal human character with arguments that go beyond the actual (corrected) preferences of individuals. The social and political grounds of these arguments are presented mainly in Chapter III of *On Liberty* and Chapter III of *Representative Government*.[48]

Justification of an ideal human character is the initial step of the educative argument in *Representative Government*. Mill sets out to show, first, that the active character is best for individuals and for society and, then (in the second step, which I discuss in the next section), that democratic participation best favors the development of that kind of character. The "active character" is one "which struggles against evils . . . [and] which endeavours to make circumstances bend to itself."[49] In *On Liberty*, where Mill offers the most extensive and eloquent portrait of this type of character, the originality and even eccentricity of the active character receive more emphasis; the value of liberty at times appears to depend crucially on a few geniuses.[50] But since in *Representative Government* he is arguing for widespread participation, he must concentrate on features of the active character that could plausibly be developed in large numbers of citizens. Here the individual model for the active character becomes chiefly the person who strives "to improve his circumstances," and the social model becomes the "striving, go-ahead character of England and the United States."[51] Despite Mill's scorn for Calvinism, this achievement ethic that he finds in England

[48] For the ethical bases of these arguments, see below, Chapter 2, pp. 55-63.

[49] *CRG*, ch. III, p. 59.

[50] *Liberty*, ch. III, pp. 107-9, 115-21. Also see "On Genius," *Monthly Repository* 6 (Oct. 1832), pp. 649-59.

[51] *CRG*, ch. III, pp. 61, 63-64.

and the United States resembles the Protestant ethic to which Weber attributed the rise of capitalism. But Mill here sees only "self-denial" in Calvinism, ignoring Calvin's worldly injunctions ("let us not cease to strive").[52] While therefore rejecting a religious foundation for the achievement ethic, Mill assigns that ethic a major role in social and economic progress—scarcely any less significant than that Weber was to ascribe to the Protestant ethic.

To show that an active national character better promotes social progress, Mill compares the English and the French characters:

> [W]henever anything goes amiss, the habitual impulse of French people is to say, 'Il faut de la patience;' and of English people, 'What a shame.' The people who think it a shame when anything goes wrong—who rush to the conclusion that the evil could and ought to have been prevented, are those who, in the long run, do most to make the world better.[53]

Like many of his contemporaries, Mill came close to accepting national stereotypes, writing as if the character of the French miners in the north (for example) were identical to that of the shopkeepers of Paris. Many social scientists now accept the idea of a national character

---

[52] *Liberty*, ch. III, pp. 111-13. However, Mill does credit Protestantism with cultivating "active minds" and spreading education to lower classes (*Auguste Comte and Positivism*, in *CW*, vol. X, pp. 321-22). Cf. John Calvin, *Institutes of the Christian Religion*, tr. John Allen, Philadelphia, 1936, vol. I, pp. 786-90; and Max Weber, *The Protestant Ethic and the Spirit of Capitalism*, tr. Talcott Parsons, New York, 1958, pp. 47-78, 98-128.

[53] *CRG*, ch. III, p. 64. Cf. "Centralisation," *Edinburgh Review* 115 (April 1862), p. 350.

but, to avoid the implication that society is undifferentiated, refer to "modal" personalities or characters. The evidence for distinctive national characters is stronger with respect to differences in customs and norms than it is with respect to differences in types of personalities.[54]

That the national character of the United States emphasizes achievement more than that of most other modern industrial nations is widely accepted now (though some sociologists in the 1950s claimed to notice a decline in the values of achievement in this country). The comparative absence of rigid distinctions of status, as Mill and Tocqueville foresaw, has encouraged Americans to seek material success as a way of securing status.[55] Britain, too, has "come to accept the values of achievement in its economic and educational system and to some extent in its political system," while retaining more of the traditional ascriptive values longer than Mill and

[54] H.C.J. Duijker and N. H. Frijda, *National Character and National Stereotypes*, Amsterdam, 1960, pp. 14, 17, 21, 29, 31-36. Also see Don Martindale (ed.), *National Character in the Perspective of the Social Sciences*, The Annals 370 (March 1967); and Alex Inkeles and Daniel J. Levinson, "National Character: The Study of Modal Personality and Socio-Cultural Systems," in Gardner Lindzey and Elliot Aronson (eds.), *The Handbook of Social Psychology*, 2d ed., Reading, Mass., 1969, vol. IV, pp. 418-506.

[55] Seymour Martin Lipset, *The First New Nation*, New York, 1963, pp. 101-6, 132-33. Also see Lipset and Leo Lowenthal (eds.), *Culture and Social Character: The Work of David Riesman Reviewed*, New York, 1961; Clyde Kluckhohn, "Have There Been Any Discernible Shifts in American Values During the Past Generation?" in Elting E. Morison (ed.), *The American Style*, New York, 1958, pp. 145-217; and Fred Greenstein, "New Light on Changing American Values: A Forgotten Body of Survey Data," *Social Forces* 42 (May 1964), pp. 441-50. The references to Tocqueville and Mill are, respectively, *De la démocratie en Amérique*, Paris, 1951, vol. II, Pt. II, ch. 13, pp. 181-86; and "Tocqueville," in *DD*, pp. 131-36.

Tocqueville would have expected. Despite the persisting differences between England and the United States in this respect, achievement, it is usually said, remains a more salient characteristic of their national characters than it does of the French.[56]

If these differences in national character exist, are they associated with social progress? As Leslie Stephen pointed out, it is very difficult to disentangle the various causes of social progress even if we have a clear notion of what constitutes social progress. Stephen asked: "Are the institutions really the cause or the effect? Has the energy of the English race made their institutions free? or have the free institutions made them energetic? or are the institutions and the character collateral effects of a great variety of causes?"[57] We may never be able to answer these questions satisfactorily. Indeed, few modern studies even address themselves to these questions, and the best known one that considers certain aspects of them, McClelland's *The Achieving Society*, is not conclusive. McClelland examined the themes in children's stories in some thirty countries, the responses of business executives and professionals in four countries, and the literature and folklore of several kinds of societies. He found that the frequency with which achievement themes appear in this material is related positively to economic growth. For example, a high level of achievement imagery in children's stories is related to a high level of economic growth thirty years later (when the

[56] Lipset, *First New Nation*, pp. 123, 213, 215-16, 224-32, 259-61. Also see Stanley Hoffmann (ed.), *In Search of France*, Cambridge, Mass., 1963; and Richard Rose, "England: A Traditionally Modern Political Culture," in Lucian W. Pye and Sidney Verba (eds.), *Political Culture and Political Development*, Princeton, 1965, pp. 83-129.
[57] Stephen, *Utilitarians*, p. 277.

children had become adults). Even if we believe that ¯ McClelland's indices measure genuine social attitudes (and this conclusion is certainly questionable), we cannot say that his findings exclude other causes of economic growth, or even establish achievement motivation itself as a cause. The most that can be said is that the findings are consistent with Mill's proposition that achievement-oriented societies tend to exhibit more economic progress than other societies.[58]

In any case, the alleged connection between attitudes of achievement and economic growth is only a small part of Mill's argument. For economic growth cannot alone generate the intellectual and moral improvement that is the most important component of Mill's idea of social progress. Indeed, Mill neither expects nor desires economic growth to continue indefinitely.[59] Moreover, economic achievement may even distract a society from the more important goals of intellectual and moral development. Mill agrees with Tocqueville that in American society "a vast energy of passion . . . is developed and squandered in the petty advancements in fortune, and the hurried snatching of petty pleasures."[60] But Mill argues that it is not the energy or the emphasis on achievement that is to blame for this squandering; rather, it is the exclusive direction of that energy toward material gain. The immediate result of the achievement ethic may be the extension of men's power over merely

[58] David C. McClelland, *The Achieving Society*, New York, 1961, pp. 71-105, 107-58, 259-66. More generally, see John W. Atkinson and Norman T. Feather (eds.), *A Theory of Achievement Motivation*, New York, 1966; Heinz Heckhausen, *The Anatomy of Achievement Motivation*, New York, 1967; and M. D. Vernon, *Human Motivation*, Cambridge, Eng., 1969, pp. 121-28.
[59] See Chapter 4, below, pp. 162-63.
[60] "Tocqueville," in *DD*, pp. 134-35.

material resources, but this consequence, Mill thinks, can create some of the prerequisites for moral and intellectual development.[61] Because a national character oriented toward economic achievement does not automatically produce nobler moral and intellectual qualities, Mill insists that other conditions, particularly social and political institutions that foster participation, are necessary to direct the achieving spirit into more worthy channels.

Mill anticipates another objection to his idea of an achieving society—that active, striving individuals are apt to envy others who are more successful than they are. Mill doubts that this envy is likely; on the contrary, a person "bestirring himself with hopeful prospects to improve his circumstances, is the one who feels goodwill toward others . . . who have succeeded in, the same pursuit."[62] Sociologists now discuss the attitudes people have toward the status or class of other people under the rubric of "relative deprivation," which is meant to be neutral between envy (unjustified feelings of disapproval) and false consciousness (unjustified feelings of approval). A person is relatively deprived of some good when he wants but does not have it, sees other persons having it, and believes in the feasibility of his having it.[63] If recent studies of relative deprivation are any guide, Mill was only too correct in his belief that achieving societies are relatively free of envy. In a study of relative deprivation in England, W. G. Runciman found few manifestations of envy among his respondents. Indeed, manual workers, whom some of Mill's contemporaries

[61] *CRG*, ch. III, p. 64, and "Tocqueville," in *DD*, p. 148.
[62] *CRG*, ch. III, p. 61.
[63] W. G. Runciman, *Relative Deprivation and Social Justice*, London, 1966, pp. 9-12.

expected to be the most discontented, feel less relatively deprived than nonmanual workers. Lower-status persons apparently compare their current positions with what they had before, rather than with positions of groups or persons above them.[64] In light of the gross discrepancies in class and status that still persist in these societies, the worry should be not excessive envy but unwarranted contentment. Mill was responding to the fear that the working classes would demand more than their due—the fear, in Macaulay's deliberately exaggerated prophecy, that working-class suffrage would bring about the end of "literature, science, commerce" and that "a few half-naked fishermen would divide with the owls and foxes the ruins of the greatest European cities."[65] Having attended to allaying these fears, Mill felt no need to concern himself with the opposite threat. To this extent he shared a prejudice of his age.

PARTICIPATION AND CIVIC EDUCATION

The second part of the educative argument is intended to show that "government of the many" is more likely to foster an active kind of character than "government of the one or the few." Unlike democracy, monarchy

[64] Runciman, pp. 193, 198, 204-5, 294. Cf. Robert E. Lane, *Political Ideology*, New York, 1962, esp. pp. 67-68.
[65] Macaulay, p. 314. Here Macaulay carefully avoided endorsing this conclusion himself, asserting only that it follows from James Mill's premises. But elsewhere Macaulay's own view in fact came close to this conclusion: the first use which the people will make of universal suffrage "will be to plunder every man in the kingdom who has a good coat on his back and a good roof over his head" (*Speeches and Poems*, New York, 1867, vol. 1, p. 317). Cf. James Fitzjames Stephen, *Liberty, Equality, Fraternity*, Cambridge, Eng., 1967, p. 80; and Leslie Stephen, "Social Macadamisation," *Fraser's Magazine* n.s. 6 (Aug. 1872), p. 150.

and aristocracy by their very natures discourage citizens from taking part in politics and thus fail to reap the educative fruits of participation. Again, Mill argues from the case apparently most favorable to his opponents —a benevolent monarchy or aristocracy—but this time with a twist. Since a benevolent ruler may satisfy the needs of his subjects so completely that they are lulled into passivity, benevolent monarchies and aristocracies, as instruments of civic education, may be even worse than malevolent ones.[66]

At this stage of the argument Mill adopts a more specifically political concept of the active character. No longer does he refer chiefly to the values of a diffuse achievement ethic; now he focuses on the intellectual and moral qualities that an active character should exhibit in political life. This move forces him to show that participation contributes to these specific qualities. It also compels him to go beyond the earlier contrast between active and passive societies, since active societies do not necessarily channel their achieving spirit into moral and intellectual improvement in political life. The significant contrast in Mill's mind now becomes one between a society in which individuals pursue their material interests in private life and a society in which citizens seek civic values in public life.

Mill points to three educative consequences of participation, which together define the ideal active character: (1) a sense of citizenship that makes citizens feel "under no other external restraint than the necessities of nature, or mandates of society which he has his share in imposing, and which it is open to him, if he thinks them wrong, publicly to dissent from, and exert himself actively to get altered"; (2) a largeness of "conceptions"

[66] *CRG*, ch. III, pp. 45-49, 64-65.

and "sentiments," which extends citizens' thoughts and feelings beyond the "satisfaction of daily wants"; and (3) an understanding of the general interest and stimulation of public-regarding attitudes.[67] This last consequence, the most important for Mill, comprises the "moral part of the instruction afforded by the participation of the private citizen":

> He is called upon, while so engaged, to weigh interests not his own; to be guided, in case of conflicting claims, by another rule than his private partialities; to apply, at every turn, principles and maxims which have for their reason of existence the common good: and he usually finds associated with him in the same work minds more familiarized than his own with these ideas and operations, whose study it will be to supply reasons to his understanding, and stimulation to his feeling for the general interest.[68]

In his *Autobiography* Mill reveals that he also believed efforts to increase participation would, as a political tactic, stimulate civic education. As the majority were granted more political power, the privileged minority would have a greater incentive to promote their political education.[69]

For empirical support of his claim for the three educative consequences of participation, Mill refers to the high quality of the speeches in ancient Athens and the characteristics of American citizens as described by

---

[67] *CRG*, ch. III, pp. 66-69; and "Tocqueville," in *DD*, pp. 101-5. Mill's arguments (and some of his language) closely resemble those of James Mackintosh in "Universal Suffrage," *Edinburgh Review* 31 (Dec. 1818), pp. 179-80.

[68] *CRG*, ch. III, p. 68.

[69] *Autobiography*, ch. V, pp. 103-4.

Tocqueville. But Mill considers all of this to be only indirect and preliminary evidence, since neither Athens nor the United States satisfies his criteria for an ideal form of government.[70] For the same reason, evidence drawn from modern democracies cannot be conclusive either. But if, under conditions far from ideal, participation still appears to have some educative effect, Mill's claim would be strengthened. Recent studies in fact lend some credence to the claim.

The sense of citizenship that Mill links to participation corresponds to what social scientists now call a sense of political efficacy—the feeling that one's "vote counts in the operation of government" and that "there are other reasonable ways in which [one] can influence the progress of the system." The sense of efficacy positively correlates with participation, even when many other variables are held constant. It is higher in the United States and United Kingdom than it is in Germany, Italy, and Mexico, where opportunities for participation are less extensive. Participation and the sense of efficacy probably reinforce each other: the more a citizen participates, the more confident he or she becomes about participating in the future.[71]

Participation is also associated with greater political knowledge, which is part of what Mill means by a "largeness of conceptions." If participation as it currently prevails does not make an "educated man" (and Mill promises this happy result only when the "amount of public duty assigned to him [is] considerable"), active partici-

---

[70] CRG, ch. VIII, pp. 164-67.
[71] Pateman, pp. 45-50; Campbell et al., pp. 515-19: Robert A. Dahl, Who Governs? New Haven, 1961, pp. 287-88; Gabriel Almond and Sidney Verba, The Civic Culture, Princeton, 1963, pp. 231, 236, 238-39, 243.

pants are nevertheless more likely to have more sophisticated opinions, to be better informed about politics, and to be better able to perceive differences between parties and candidates than are less active citizens.[72] No causal connection between participation and this kind of civic education has been firmly established—largely because it is so hard to distinguish the effect of formal education from the effect of participation, with which it is highly correlated. But as with the sense of efficacy and participation, political knowledge and participation are probably mutually reinforcing.

It is still more difficult to determine whether greater participation encourages a stronger commitment to the general interest. One of the few modern studies that bear on this question found that voters in higher-status groups tend to be more public-regarding than voters in lower-status groups. The former are more likely than the latter to vote for expenditures for public projects (such as parks), even though they would have to pay more taxes and probably would not benefit as much from the projects as would the other groups.[73] Since the higher-status groups participate more than lower-status

[72] Ronald Inglehart, *The Silent Revolution*, Princeton, 1976, ch. 10; Campbell et al., pp. 250-53; Lester Milbrath, *Political Participation*, Chicago, 1965, pp. 64-65; Key, pp. 185-86; and Frank Bealey, Jean Blondel, and W. P. McCann, *Constituency Politics*, London, 1965, p. 237. The quotation from Mill is in *CRG*, ch. III, p. 67.

[73] James Q. Wilson and Edward Banfield, "Public-Regardingness as a Value Premise in Voting Behavior," *American Political Science Review* 58 (Dec. 1964), pp. 876-87. Also see Campbell et al., pp. 195-96. Wilson and Banfield have been sharply criticized, chiefly for their claims about ethnicity; see, e.g. Raymond E. Wolfinger and John Osgood Field, "Political Ethos and the Structure of City Government," *American Political Science Review* 60 (June 1966), 306-26. Also see *American Political Science Review* 60 (Dec. 1966), pp. 998-1000.

groups, one might infer (though without much confidence and without any additional evidence) that greater participation is associated with greater concern for the public interest. If, however, a concern for the general interest did not manifest itself in electoral behavior, Mill would hardly be surprised. For he locates his "school of public spirit" not so much in the act of voting as in the activities of political associations where individuals can learn from each other by discussing the means and ends of political action.[74]

Mill does not deny that the act of voting has some educative value:

> People think it fanciful to expect so much from what seems so slight a cause—to recognise a potent instrument of mental improvement in the exercise of political franchises by manual labourers. Yet unless substantial mental cultivation in the mass of mankind is to be a mere vision, this is the road by which it must come.[75]

But he also insists that an act done only "once in a few years, and for which nothing in the daily habits of the citizen has prepared him, leaves his intellect and his moral dispositions very much as it found them."[76] Participation in national politics (which is mainly electoral) must therefore be supplemented by vigorous political activity in local government, which along with jury duty and free discussion is the chief instrument of the public education of citizens.[77] Because the scale of

[74] CRG, ch. III, p. 68.
[75] CRG, ch. VIII, pp. 164-65.
[76] "Tocqueville," in DD, pp. 100-101. Mill here is referring to the infrequent elections for the Council of State in post-Revolutionary France.
[77] CRG, ch. XV, p. 276; ch. VI, pp. 109-10.

41

local politics is small, citizens have more opportunities to take part in actual governing and also can acquire a greater sense of responsibility for their actions and a more immediate interest in the outcome of political decisions.[78] That turnout in local elections is lower than in national elections in most democracies does not undermine Mill's belief. Local elections at present tend to be less competitive and receive less attention from the mass media and from party organizations. More important, a recent analysis of the Almond and Verba data indicates that the understanding of issues, the sense of effectiveness, and the frequency of reported attempts to influence government are greater with respect to local than national government in England, the United States, Germany, Italy, and Mexico.[79]

Mill elsewhere carries his argument a step further and urges democratic participation in industry. "If . . . mankind is to continue to improve," industry must be based on "the association of the labourers themselves on terms of equality, collectively owning the capital with which they carry on their operations, and working under managers elected and removable by themselves."[80] This proposal loomed large in later socialist thought and has

[78] CRG, ch. xv, p. 276; ch. vi, pp. 109-10. A seemingly similar claim for local politics is made by Joseph Schumpeter (p. 260), who has been called an "elitist theorist of democracy," but he does not consider the educative effects of participation at all.

[79] Robert A. Dahl and Edward R. Tufte, Size and Democracy, Stanford, 1973, pp. 54, 58, 59-60. Also see Almond and Verba, pp. 80-82, 185, 188; Robert E. Agger, Daniel Goldrich, and Bert E. Swanson, The Rulers and the Ruled, New York, 1964, pp. 624-25; and Robert A. Dahl, Democracy in the United States, Chicago, 1972, pp. 235-38.

[80] Political Economy, Bk. iv, ch. vii, § 6, p. 775. This chapter was substantially revised in the third edition (1852), resulting in this more favorable view of workers' cooperatives.

recently been revived by critics of those democratic theories that neglect the importance of increased participation. There is growing evidence that democratic participation at the place of work does have some of the educative consequences for which Mill hoped.[81]

Because Mill insisted on the necessity of a vigorous political life at the local level, it would be a mistake to cite the low levels of political information that prevail in most modern democracies as evidence that Mill exaggerated the educative effects of participation. Most democracies have not yet come close to meeting the high standards Mill set for participation in local government, private associations, and industry. Political participation can educate citizens only if it becomes a part of their daily life.

The analysis of the educative consequences of participation so far presented does not completely capture the import of Mill's conception of civic education. His conception has certain features, particularly an ambiguity between political and intellectual education, that can be more fully brought out through a comparison with Rousseau. Such a comparison also will underscore the extent to which Mill's commitment to participation goes beyond that of a theorist noted for his participatory zeal.

There are, as has been observed, some striking similarities between Mill's view of the educative function of participation and Rousseau's view.[82] Just as a chief aim of participation for Mill is to turn the minds of citizens from private to public interests, so Rousseau's

[81] Pateman (esp. pp. 67-102) helpfully relates this evidence to democratic theory. For a survey of the empirical literature, see Paul Blumberg, *Industrial Democracy*, London, 1968.

[82] See, e.g., Pateman, pp. 29-30.

aim is to transform the particular wills of individuals into a general will. When Mill demands that a citizen be "guided . . . by another rule than his private partialities" and that he apply "principles and maxims which have for their reason of existence the common good," he echoes Rousseau's injunction to citizens to consider the general will instead of their particular preferences when voting on a proposal in the assembly.[83] If participation has sustained a proper civic education, citizens will not find this injunction hard to follow; ideally, according to both Mill and Rousseau, a citizen should feel no conflict between his private inclinations and his public duties.[84] The *process* of civic education for both theorists is also similar. Citizens cannot learn the lessons of civic education entirely on their own, even though one of those lessons is to think for themselves. Mill's civic education, like any education, requires teachers as well as students.[85] If no citizen stands above another as a political teacher in Rousseau's republic, that is because the most effective teacher of all—the Lawgiver—has done his work well.[86] Mill and Rousseau further agree that all education, especially education in social and political life, requires the experience of testing principles in practice. In Mill's words, "action can only be learnt in action"; as "we do not learn to read or write . . . by being merely told how to do it, but by doing it," so we learn

[83] *CRG*, ch. III, p. 68; Rousseau, *Contrat social*, Bk. IV, ch. II, p. 106.

[84] *CRG*, ch. III, p. 68; Rousseau, *Contrat social*, Bk. I, ch. VIII, p. 36; Bk. II, ch. I, p. 40; Bk. III, ch. II, pp. 69-70; and *Émile*, tr. Barbara Foxley, London, 1948, Bk. I, p. 7.

[85] *CRG*, ch. XV, pp. 282, 294. In his *Inaugural Address at St. Andrews*, Mill says that "what we require to be taught on [politics], is to be our own teachers" (in *DD*, vol. IV, pp. 381-82).

[86] *Contrat social*, Bk. II, ch. VII, pp. 51-54.

how to exercise political power in a democracy only by practicing it.[87] This emphasis on learning by doing is one reason why both theorists denounce passive character. Both see Christianity as a principal source of passivity; although Mill (unlike Rousseau) believes that Christianity and other religions can overcome this tendency, he much prefers the more activist Religion of Humanity.[88] Rousseau goes to much greater lengths than Mill in devising ways to eradicate passivity in his citizenry and the *amour-propre* that accompanies it: games, festivals, patriotic festivals, didactic theater, and military parades unceasingly occupy citizens in public activity.[89]

Despite these similarities, virtually all of Mill's own references to Rousseau are unfavorable—at times even scornful. Mill regards Rousseau as the apostle of a "philosophy of nature" that would remake citizens according to a model of the noble savage. The "predominant ingredient" in Rousseau's thought is a doctrine that proclaims the "Divinity of Nature" and sets up "its fancied dictates as an authoritative rule of action." The

[87] Mill, "Tocqueville," in *DD*, p. 102; "De Tocqueville on Democracy in America" (hereafter cited as "Tocqueville" [1835]), *London Review* 2 (Oct. 1835), p. 100; *Inaugural Address*, pp. 381-82; *CRG*, ch. III, p. 52; *Liberty*, ch. II, pp. 68-69, ch. III, pp. 100-101, 107; and Rousseau, *Émile*, Bk. II, p. 64; Bk. III, pp. 143-44.

[88] *Contrat social*, Bk. IV, ch. VIII, pp. 128-31; *CRG*, ch. III, pp. 60-61; and *Three Essays on Religion* ("Utility of Religion"), in *CW*, vol. X, pp. 403-28.

[89] *Contrat social*, Bk. III, ch. XV, pp. 95-96; *Économie politique*, in *Political Writings*, vol. I, pp. 248-50, 255-57; *Projet de constitution pour la Corse*, in *Political Writings*, vol. II, pp. 344-46; *Considérations sur le gouvernement de Pologne*, in *Political Writings*, vol. II, ch. XII, pp. 491-92; and *Politics and the Arts: Letter to M. d'Alembert on the Theatre* (hereafter cited as *Letter to d'Alembert*), tr. Allan Bloom, Glencoe, 1960, pp. 67-68, 125-26.

standard of nature is either meaningless when it refers to nature's physical and mental laws, which men cannot help but follow, or irrational and immoral when it refers to "things as they would be, apart from human intervention." Whatever good exists in the world comes from the efforts of human beings to *amend* the spontaneous course of nature, for nature is "replete with everything which when committed by human beings is most worthy of abhorrence."[90] Actually, Rousseau would quite agree that natural man is ignorant and lacking in virtue; moreover, Rousseau does not think men can return to the state of nature, and he usually maintains that, on balance, social life offers possibilities for virtue that exceed the advantages of primitive life.[91] Nature, to be sure, is a guide for Rousseau, but it operates through artifice and suggests a model of citizenship as far removed from primitive life as Mill's model is. The means by which the independence of natural man is approximated in society are distinctly artificial institutions that make citizens depend excessively on the law and the state, rather than on other specific individuals.[92]

Although Mill's reading of Rousseau on this point is misleading, Mill's suspicion that Rousseau has in mind a political vision very much at odds with his own is entirely correct. The similarities we have noticed are overshadowed by profound differences in their views of both the ends and means of civic education. The goal of civic

[90] Mill, *Three Essays on Religion* ("Nature"), pp. 376, 395, 401-2; "Coleridge," p. 123; *Comte*, pp. 299, 304 (all in *CW*, vol. x). Two vaguely favorable references to Rousseau are in "Bentham," p. 110, and *Liberty*, ch. II, p. 85.

[91] *Contrat social*, Bk. I, ch. VIII, p. 36; and *Discours sur l'origine et les fondements de l'inégalité parmi les hommes*, in *Political Writings*, vol. I, p. 207.

[92] *Émile*, Bk. II, p. 49; and *Contrat social*, Bk. II, ch. VII, pp. 51-52, ch. XII, p. 63.

education for Mill is not only the creation of a public-regarding spirit but also the development of critical intelligence and extensive knowledge in citizens. To attain this goal necessitates an inegalitarian recognition of superior intelligence that Mill consistently recommends and the diversity of opinions and "experiments in living" that *On Liberty* in particular prescribes.[93] While Rousseau also expects conflicting interests in his society (otherwise "we should hardly be conscious of a common interest"), the salient feature of his republic is consensus: the closer that public opinion comes to unanimity, the more the general will is realized.[94] As for the intellectual development of citizens, Rousseau writes that "in a properly constituted state, men are so busy that they have no time for speculation. They are so equal that none gains preference as more learned or shrewd."[95] It is the patriotic rather than the enlightened citizen who is the nucleus of Rousseau's republic; the corrupting influence of an intellectual elite, symbolized by the typical philosopher, must be avoided at all costs. Whereas Mill believes that reason stimulates a concern for the general interest, Rousseau insists that reason is the supreme instrument of rationalization, permitting men to justify preferring themselves to others.[96]

[93] *Liberty*, ch. III, pp. 101-2, 106-7. Mill did, however, believe that the elimination of extreme inequalities in material resources was necessary for education (see *Political Economy*, Bk. II, ch. xiii, § 3, p. 375).

[94] *Contrat social*, Bk. II, ch. III, p. 42; Bk. IV, chs. I-II, VII, pp. 102-6, 122-23; *Letter to d'Alembert*, pp. 59-61.

[95] *"Préface" à Narcisse*, in *Oeuvres complètes*, Paris, 1959, vol. II, p. 965.

[96] *Discours sur . . . l'inégalité*, pp. 161-62; *Discours. Si le rétablissement des sciences et des arts à contribué à épurer les moeurs*, in *Oeuvres complètes*, Paris, 1905, vol. I, pp. 10-20; and *Économie politique*, p. 241.

As the ends of civic education diverge for Rousseau and Mill, so the means for achieving them differ. The difference, however, is not captured by a contrast between representative government and direct democracy, for Rousseau endorses "elective aristocracy" as the best form of government. Even though this aristocracy embraces the idea of popular sovereignty, as well as some practices we associate with direct democracy (such as an assembly of all citizens voting on general laws), the actual scope for substantive political participation in Rousseau's republic is modest. The periodic assemblies of the people decide primarily whether to retain the present form of government and the current members of the government.[97] When exercising their irrevocable right of sovereignty, the people confine themselves to the "simple act of voting." The right of speaking, proposing, dividing, and debating belongs exclusively to the government, along with great discretion in most matters of government, including the power to declare war.[98] Absent are even the tempered opportunities that Mill provides for national political discussion in the legislature and in electoral campaigns. In private associations and in local politics (the most appropriate point of comparison in terms of scale), Mill offers much more. Thus, with respect to substantive political discourse, Rousseau portrays a political life markedly less participatory than that which Mill favors.

Compared to the cautious optimism of Mill, Rousseau's prognosis for civic education is bleak. Despite the heroic efforts of the Lawgiver and the strenuous participation of citizens in public activities, particular wills

[97] *Contrat social,* Bk. III, ch. V, p. 75, ch. XIII, p. 93, ch. XVIII, pp. 101-2.
[98] *Contrat social,* Bk. IV, ch. I, p. 104; Bk. II, ch. II, p. 41.

inevitably encroach upon the general will. Even the best republics degenerate, for civic education is ultimately powerless against *amour-propre*.[99] Mill, too, sees "an incessant and ever-flowing current of human affairs towards the worse," but he believes that with great "exertions," encouraged by civic education, men can restrain this current of history.[100] These exertions can be effective because Mill's theory of development attributes to ideas and reason an influence sufficient to overcome retrogressive passions and interests. For Rousseau, reason at best enables men to understand history; it cannot contain historical decay.

Mill thus allows more scope for participation and holds out more hope for improvement than does Rousseau, but his conception of civic education is also more ambiguous. Describing the goals of participation, he often vacillates between political education and intellectual education, evidently assuming that the development of general critical intelligence and extensive knowledge accompanies the growth of political skill and political knowledge. Yet Mill offers little reason to believe that for most citizens this general intellectual education is a likely result of political participation or that, indeed, it is even necessary (beyond a minimal level) for effective participation. If Rousseau underestimates the value of intellectual enlightenment, he is not obviously wrong in thinking that a perfectly respectable citizenry may flourish with relatively meager intellectual attainments, and that political activity itself

[99] *Contrat social*, Bk. III, ch. x, pp. 88-91. On the theme of degeneration in Rousseau's thought, see Judith N. Shklar, *Men and Citizens*, Cambridge, Eng., 1969, esp. pp. 159-60, 183, 206-8; and Bertrand de Jouvenal, "Rousseau, the Pessimistic Evolutionist," *Yale French Studies* 28 (1961-62), pp. 83-96.

[100] *CRG*, ch. II, pp. 26-27.

will teach little more than political skills, knowledge, and loyalty. Mill does not fully face up to these possibilities because he disregards any distinction between political and intellectual education.

However ambiguous the nature of civic education in Mill's theory may be, Mill's commitment to an educative aim in politics never wavers. Armed with arguments for the educative efficacy of participation, he takes on all objections to the democratization of political life. If the members of the working class do not yet qualify as ideal citizens, the experience of participation will bring them closer to this ideal. Democracy itself is the "remedy for the worst mischiefs to which a democratic state of society is exposed."[101] This would be part of Mill's reply to present-day democratic theorists who fear greater participation because of the alleged ignorance and illiberality of inactive citizens.[102] However, so long as an alternative to more extensive participation exists—specifically, the exclusion of these less competent citizens either by prohibiting their entry into politics or by refusing to encourage it—Mill's educative argument is not sufficient. Why take the risk that civic education might fail? Mill's answer, following Tocqueville, is that "democracy, in the modern world, is inevitable."[103] It is prudent to prepare for this inevitability now by introducing the less active citizens to the responsibilities of political life. Mill thus shifts the burden of risk to the opponents of more extensive participation.

[101] "Tocqueville," in *DD*, pp. 135-36.

[102] See Dennis F. Thompson, *The Democratic Citizen*, Cambridge, Eng., 1970, pp. 67-72 and the citations there.

[103] "Tocqueville," in *DD*, pp. 85-86. Although the growing "equality of conditions" does not necessarily bring about democracy, it does "naturally tend to produce" it, according to Mill.

Some contemporary critics of "democratic elitism" have revived a form of Mill's argument. They point out that the elite consensus on which the elitists pin their hopes cannot prevent the intrusion of masses into politics. If the masses are as ignorant and illiberal as the elitists claim, they are vulnerable to demagogic movements. The permanent limitation of participation, therefore, is not a live option. We can have either greater participation where citizens are at the mercy of irresponsible politicians or greater participation where citizens are educated to act responsibly.[104]

Universal suffrage has come to modern democracies, but the levels of participation fall below what Mill hoped for. He perhaps would not have been surprised at this eventuality, once he had grasped the limited nature of the opportunities for political influence and the gross discrepancies in resources that now exist among citizens. However, he did not seriously consider the problem of how to activate an inactive citizenry. Along with most of his contemporaries, he assumed that the desire for a greater share of political power was so strong among the unenfranchised that, once granted the rights of citizenship, they would eagerly exercise them. To be sure, Mill foresaw, with Tocqueville, a danger as democracy advances "not of too great liberty but of too ready submission, not of anarchy but of servility, not of too rapid change but of Chinese stationariness."[105] But although in *Representative Government* he still takes Tocqueville's fears seriously, he really offers only institutional opportunities for citizens who wish to participate, not means for stimulating a desire to participate. He concentrates on the more immediate problem of

[104] See, e.g., Bachrach, pp. 45-46.
[105] "Tocqueville," in *DD*, p. 135.

how to convince the enfranchised to support wider participation, not how to persuade the unenfranchised to take advantage of so obvious a benefit.

The formative years of *Representative Government* were years of lively agitation by citizens who had been denied political rights. Not only the middle class but also the working class began to play an active part in the various reform movements and numerous agitations of the period. The growing political activity of the working class—as in the Chartist movement—created severe tensions between working-class groups and Mill's usual allies, the Philosophic Radicals, who resisted the idea that working-class interests could conflict with middle-class interests. The Philosophic Radicals struggled to channel working-class political activity, which they found already energetic enough, into a more broadly based radical movement. They certainly did not want to see more participation that merely reinforced class divisions, and for this reason they were uncomfortable also with the largely middle-class Anti-Corn Law movement.[106] Later, well after the Philosophic Radicals had effectively collapsed as a political force, Mill took part in several mass meetings of workers demanding more extensive political rights. According to a contemporary newspaper account, a crowd of "tens of thousands" of workers—a "teeming and swaying multitude"—listened to Mill speak in the aftermath of the Hyde Park demonstrations of 1866.[107] Although these particular encounters took place a few years after

[106] Hamburger, pp. 250-64.
[107] Michael St. John Packe, *The Life of John Stuart Mill*, London, 1954, pp. 458-63. In 1859 Mill observed that the working-class movement was quiescent, but he fully expected a resurgence ("Recent Writers," p. 62).

Representative Government was written, they reveal a political climate that, in only a slightly less extreme form, must have influenced Mill as he conceived his arguments for participation. Such a climate hardly encouraged him to worry about how to arouse a desire for participation among citizens.

The affirmation that participation educates citizens is not Mill's only response to those who fear democracy. However successful participation may be in promoting civic education, some citizens will remain more competent than others in political matters, and any satisfactory theory of democracy has to make provision for recognizing that superiority. Even if the principle of participation were fully justified, a theory of democracy must be tempered with a principle of competence. The question of whether this constraint on the principle of participation leaves citizens with any effective voice in politics can be answered only by an examination of the role of the idea of competence in Mill's theory and the structure of the political institutions that he recommends.

2

The Principle of Competence

The principle of competence expresses Mill's belief that a democracy should give as much weight as possible to superior intelligence and virtue in the political process.[1] Ideally, greater participation would realize the aim of the principle of competence by making all citizens competent, but realistically Mill recognizes that special provisions must be made so that competence gets its due in the present operation and the future development of a democracy. Mill does not think that such provisions alter the "fundamentally democratic" character of a constitution; indeed, they are needed to sustain democratic participation itself.[2] And he places strict limits on the way in which the competent minority may exercise authority.

The structure of the argument for the principle of competence matches that of the argument for the principle of participation. Paralleling the protective argument for participation is Mill's exposition of the dangers of incompetence against which democracy must protect itself. Corresponding to the educative argument for participation is an account of the proper role of the competent minority in the political education of citizens.

[1] *CRG*, ch. v, pp. 106-7; ch. vi, p. 118; ch. vii, pp. 144-45, 151-52; ch. viii, p. 173; ch. xii, p. 232; and *Liberty*, ch. iii, p. 119.

[2] "Bentham," p. 109; and *CRG*, ch. vi, pp. 115-16.

Mill's arguments implicitly employ two kinds of competence—instrumental and moral. Instrumental competence is the ability to discover the best means to certain ends and the ability to identify ends that satisfy individuals' interests as they perceive them. Moral competence is the ability to discern ends that are intrinsically superior for individuals and society. Morally competent leaders are able to recognize the general interest and resist the sinister interests that dwell not only in the government but also in the democratic majority. Although the two kinds of competence do not necessarily go together, Mill does not always clearly distinguish them since ideally he would like all political leaders to exhibit both kinds. Usually he views the executive (especially the bureaucracy) as the custodian of instrumental competence and the legislature as the protector of moral competence. But the dangers of incompetence lurk everywhere, and representative democracy must mobilize its full resources to combat them.

GROUNDS OF COMPETENCE

Both the protective and the educative arguments for the principle of competence rest on a prior justification of competence Mill takes for granted in *Representative Government* but explains in *Utilitarianism*, published in serial form at the same time. Mill does not bother to justify the idea of instrumental competence, evidently assuming no one would deny that some means and ends are instrumentally better, and that some people are more skillful at discovering them. The notion of moral competence requires defense, however. To justify a political role for moral competence, Mill must show that some ends, specifically those that realize the general interest, are intrinsically superior, and for this purpose he invokes a doctrine of higher pleasures.[3] Since the ends that he has in mind are "pleasures of the intellect, feelings and imagination and moral sentiments," the doctrine has a wider and more natural application beyond political life, but at least the "moral sentiments" are needed to support a concern for the general interest, which is an essential part of competence in Mill's representative democracy.

Bentham justified the superiority of higher pleasures by identifying such features as their greater permanency, safety, and lesser cost, which cause them to yield more satisfaction for an individual in the long run than do other experiences.[4] Mill purports to believe that this argument from "circumstantial advantages" is valid and sufficient, but offers a further argument from the "intrinsic nature" of the higher pleasures.[5] This further argument, it turns out, is not gratuitous. Mill needs it because he admits that higher pleasures do not necessarily produce so much contentment as lower ones do, and may even produce more acute suffering. If higher pleasures make men happier, it is not Benthamite happiness they enjoy but a kind of happiness that may include a net balance of suffering, made bearable only by a well-developed "sense of dignity." In any case, it is not the happiness of the individual but the happiness of a whole society that is the decisive criterion: "[I]f it may be possibly doubted whether a noble character is always the happier for its nobleness, there can be no

[3] *Utilitarianism*, ch. II, p. 211.
[4] Bentham, *Introduction*, ch. IV, pp. 38-41; and Mill, *Autobiography*, ch. II, p. 30.
[5] *Utilitarianism*, ch. II, p. 211.

doubt that it makes other people happier, and that the world in general is immensely a gainer by it."[6]

The doctrine of higher pleasures is independent of Mill's proof of the principle of utility, a preoccupation of his critics and his defenders in recent years.[7] Both do appeal, in part, to actual desires of individuals to show that certain objects are desirable. But even if it is true that people desire only utility or happiness, it does not follow that people desire only higher forms of utility or happiness. And if people do not desire only happiness, it may still be true that more competent or experienced persons prefer, and ought to prefer, higher forms of happiness.

How, then, does Mill demonstrate the superiority of higher pleasures? The first step of the argument establishes who is most competent to decide:

> On a question which is the best worth having of two pleasures, or which of two modes of existence is the most grateful to the feelings, apart from its moral attributes and from its consequences, the judgment of those who are qualified by knowledge of both, or, if they differ, that of the majority among them, must be admitted as final.[8]

[6] *Utilitarianism*, ch. II, pp. 212-13. On the question of the consistency of Mill's doctrine of higher pleasures with Benthamite utilitarianism, see Anschutz, p. 18; Robson, pp. 156-57; and Maurice Mandelbaum, "On Interpreting Mill's Utilitarianism," *Journal of the History of Philosophy* 6 (Jan. 1968), p. 37.

[7] A useful collection of articles dealing with this issue is Samuel Gorovitz (ed.), *Mill: Utilitarianism*, Indianapolis, 1971; see especially the articles by Hall, Kretzmann, Margolis, and Mandelbaum.

[8] *Utilitarianism*, ch. II, pp. 213, 211.

It is, however, by no means obvious that a person can have "knowledge of both" in a way that would permit a genuine comparison between the two forms of happiness. Even if a more qualified individual once experienced a lower pleasure in the same way that the less qualified do, he can no longer regard the pleasure from the same perspective. His present judgment of that pleasure surely must be colored by the intervening experience of a life of higher pleasures if the impact of the latter on individual character is as great as Mill insists it is. How can Socrates judge what it is like to have only foolish and porcine desires? Only if a person's powers of imagination and memory were uncommonly acute would it be possible to say that he is "equally capable of appreciating and enjoying" both forms of satisfaction. Perhaps Mill assumes that some individuals possess such refined powers, but he cannot plausibly maintain that these abilities are widespread, even among an elite.

The first step of Mill's argument resembles Socrates' reasoning in his dialogue with Glaucon in Book IX of the *Republic*.[9] Distinguishing three types of persons corresponding to the three parts of the soul—the philosophic, the ambitious, and the appetitive—Socrates asks how one should decide which kind of pleasure and which kind of life are best? The philosopher is the best

---

[9] Plato, *Republic*, tr. Paul Shorey, Cambridge, Mass., 1963, Bk. IX, 580A-83B, pp. 367-81. John Rawls makes a similar argument: "Human beings enjoy the exercise of their realized capacities . . . and this enjoyment increases the more the capacity is realized, or the greater its complexity" (*A Theory of Justice*, Cambridge, Mass., 1971, p. 426). But as he suggests, in this form the argument derives more from Aristotle than from Plato. Although Rawls says that Mill comes close to stating this principle in *Utilitarianism*, the first part of the argument that Mill actually makes seems closer to that cited above in the *Republic*.

judge, Socrates answers, because the philosophic type cannot help but experience the other kinds of pleasure "from childhood on," whereas the ambitious and the appetitive types never taste "the sweetness of the pleasure of learning the true nature of things." The philosopher of course will choose the philosophic life. So far this argument from experience sounds like Mill's. But Socrates does not rest the superiority of higher pleasures primarily on the fact that the philosopher will choose them, but on an independent theory of the Good. The Good is not pleasure, but a form of knowledge, which is the realization of man's characteristic virtue.[10] Only a true philosopher, who by definition pursues knowledge of the Forms, can know the Good. If a person who appears to have philosophic competence were to choose a nonphilosophic way of life, Socrates would simply deny that such a person is a philosopher.

Mill, however, rejects such a theory of the Good because he thinks it allows no place for the virtuous but unphilosophic man like Aristeides, and more generally because he insists that knowledge, though a condition of virtue, is not equivalent to it.[11] Without a Platonic theory of the Good, Mill must rely more heavily on the actual choices made by competent persons. Therefore, the second step of his argument is an empirical claim:

> Now it is an unquestionable fact that those who are equally acquainted with, and equally capable of appreciating and enjoying, both, do give a most marked preference to the manner of existence which employs their higher faculties.[12]

[10] *Republic*, Bk. I, 347E-354C, pp. 83-107; Bk. V, 474B-480A, pp. 511-35; Bk. VI, 502C-509C, pp. 77-107.
[11] Mill, "Grote's Plato," in *DD*, vol. IV, pp. 317-18, 292-93.
[12] *Utilitarianism*, ch. II, p. 211.

At this point it might seem that Mill is arguing in a circle.[13] Higher pleasures are those chosen by competent individuals, and competent individuals are those who enjoy and appreciate higher pleasures, as proved by the fact that they choose them. But in fact Mill's test for competence is partly distinct from the actual choices made by individuals who know both kinds of satisfaction. That the test does not depend entirely on actual choices is shown by the way in which Mill handles apparent counterexamples to his doctrine. If an individual who knows both kinds of pleasures chooses lower ones, Mill deems him incompetent—*not* simply because he makes this choice, but because he suffers from weakness of will or an impaired capacity to enjoy the superior life.[14] Although Mill does not specify what would count as evidence for the existence of a weak will or an impaired capacity, such evidence could in principle be discovered independently of any failure to choose higher pleasures. Moreover, if we were to find some competent individuals (those who know both kinds of satisfaction and do not suffer weakness of will or impaired capacities) who consistently prefer inferior forms of satisfaction, Mill's doctrine would be falsified. Thus, the criterion of competence and the justification of higher pleasures are sufficiently distinct to escape the charge of circularity, although the justification still requires that competent persons generally prefer higher pleasures.

It would be very difficult in practice to decide, for any large number of people, whether choices are made under the influence of a weak will or impaired capacity. The best that we can hope for in the way of evidence for

[13] Cf. Robson, p. 157.
[14] *Utilitarianism*, ch. II, pp. 212-13.

Mill's doctrine is some indication that individuals who know both kinds of pleasure generally prefer higher ones. The satisfactions that come from the "moral sentiments," especially a concern for the general interest, are the most pertinent to Mill's political theory, and some recent studies of moral development examine the conditions under which individuals tend to evince something very like these moral sentiments. Lawrence Kohlberg and his associates interviewed children and adults in six countries, asking them to respond to various hypothetical moral situations. The investigators distinguished six stages of moral judgment or reasoning that people use—from a stage where moral rules are interpreted in terms of hedonistic rewards and punishments to the highest stage where moral rules are based on universal principles. They found that these stages are ordered so that individuals progress from one stage to the next, as they acquire the cognitive ability to comprehend the next stage. They also discovered that individuals prefer the highest stage of moral reasoning that they can comprehend.[15] These studies cannot be taken to confirm even the empirical part of Mill's doctrine because they are themselves open to criticism—for example, for relying only on responses to hypothetical questions. Yet since they evidently are the only studies that bear on Mill's doctrine, it is worth noting that their findings are consistent with Mill's general claim that

[15] James R. Rest, Elliot Turiel, and Lawrence Kohlberg, "Level of Moral Development as a Determinant of Preference and Comprehension of the Moral Judgments Made by Others," *Journal of Personality* 37 (June 1969), pp. 225-52; and James R. Rest, "The Hierarchical Nature of Moral Judgment: A Study of Patterns of Comprehension and Preference of Moral Stages," in Rest, Kohlberg, and Turiel (eds.), *Recent Research in Moral Development* (forthcoming).

persons who are acquainted with higher as well as the lower forms of moral satisfaction prefer the higher ones.[16]

If more competent individuals generally prefer higher pleasures, should other citizens therefore choose these pleasures (perhaps letting themselves be led by the more competent)? People who lack this competence may not find it so easy to make such choices. Mill sometimes writes as if it were easy—as if individuals could choose a life of higher pleasures as one selects activities for the day or items in a store. But Mill's considered view is that a person can and should elect superior forms of satisfaction only when his character is such that he can appreciate them. Mill also sometimes implies that character in this sense cannot be easily changed, at least in the short run:

> On the average, a person who cares for other people, for his country, or for mankind, is a happier man than one who does not; but of what use is it to preach this doctrine to a man who cares for nothing but his own ease, or his own pocket? He cannot care for other people if he would. . . . He would be happier if he were the kind of person who *could* so live; but he is not, and it is probably too late for him to become, that kind of person. . . .[17]

---

[16] Mill's utilitarianism seems to fall somewhere between Kohlberg's fifth and sixth stages of moral reasoning. Kohlberg's paradigm for the sixth stage is Kant's moral theory. However, the precise location of Mill's own theory does not affect the relevance of Kohlberg's evidence to Mill's claim that individuals prefer the highest moral sentiments with which they are familiar.

[17] *CRG*, ch. VI, p. 124. In the original text the second part of the quotation comes before the first part and refers to a man who mistreats his wife and children, but Mill of course intended the point to have more general application.

But Mill also believes that character is strongly shaped by social environment and that therefore, as civilization progresses, many individuals will develop the capacity for the enjoyment of superior forms of happiness and styles of life.[18] Mill's doctrine of higher pleasures and its conception of competence in this way rest ultimately on his theory of development. In the meantime, the more competent citizens ought to have enough influence in politics to protect democracy against the most serious infirmities of rule by the less competent and enough to promote the development of competence among all citizens.

DANGERS OF INCOMPETENCE

The most extended argument for the principle of competence in political life occurs in the chapter of *Representative Government* entitled "Of the Infirmities and Dangers to Which Representative Government is Liable."

> The *positive* evils and dangers of the representative, as of every other form of government, may be reduced to two heads: first, general ignorance and incapacity, or, to speak more moderately, insufficient mental qualifications, in the controlling body; secondly, the danger of its being under the influence of interests not identical with the general welfare of the community.[19]

---

[18] *Utilitarianism*, ch. III, p. 232; ch. v, p. 252; and *Logic*, Bk. VI, ch. ii, § 3, pp. 839-40.

[19] *CRG*, ch. VI, p. 110. The two "negative" infirmities—insufficient power in the executive and inadequate opportunities for civic education—are much more briefly discussed, presumably because the former is simply a consequence of one positive in-

Instrumental competence guards against the first danger, and moral competence protects against the second.

Mill rejects the conventional nineteenth-century view that monarchies and aristocracies are superior to democracies in "high mental qualifications" (or instrumental competence).[20] The immediate target of this criticism is Tocqueville, for though Mill does not mention him here in *Representative Government*, he complains elsewhere that the virtues Tocqueville "affirmed of aristocracies in general" should have been "predicated only of some particular aristocracies." The aristocracies that are competent, Mill thinks, are also those that are so narrow and insulated that they do not act in the general interest.[21] Leaders of high competence, rare enough in any form of government, appear no more or no less frequently in democracies than in other forms of government—with one exception. A bureaucratic government can make a general claim to superior instrumental competence, for "it accumulates experience, acquires well-tried and well-considered traditional maxims, and makes provision for appropriate practical knowledge in those who have the actual conduct of affairs." But one feature disqualifies it as an ideal form of government: routine. The rules and procedures by which a bureaucracy lives become rigid and inappropriate as political conditions change. Further, bureaucratic governments tend to absorb all the competence in a society into the governing body, leaving outside no groups of talent and initiative to check and to stimulate the government. Sooner or later this tendency is bound

---

firmity; and the latter, of a failure to observe the principle of participation.

[20] *CRG*, ch. VI, pp. 110-14.

[21] "Tocqueville" (1835), pp. 116-17.

to be fatal to "the mental activity and progressiveness of the body itself."[22]

Mill's general criticism of bureaucracy has been echoed in recent studies that challenge Weber's ideal of a rational, or instrumentally competent, bureaucracy.[23] Just as Mill warned that the bureaucratic virtues of salutary rules and expertise would turn into bureaucratic vices of routine and overspecialization, so modern social scientists show how characteristics of bureaucracies that are intended to encourage efficiency actually may have the opposite effect because they are typically carried to extremes. In a classic essay that set the stage for much later work on the subject, Robert Merton argues that an effective bureaucracy demands "reliability of response" and "strict devotion to duty." These demands transform administrative rules into absolutes that are no longer relative to a given set of purposes, and discourage adapting the rules to situations that were not imagined when the rules were made.[24]

While these studies give some support to Mill's apprehensions about bureaucracy in general, we must remember that Mill directs his criticisms chiefly against

[22] *CRG*, ch. VI, p. 114; and *Liberty*, ch. v, pp. 202-3. Also see *Political Economy*, Bk. v, ch. xi, §§ 3-6, pp. 939-44.

[23] Max Weber, *Wirtschaft und Gesellschaft*, Tübingen, 1956, pp. 126-27; *The Theory of Social and Economic Organization*, tr. A. M. Henderson and Talcott Parsons, Glencoe, Ill., 1947, pp. 329-40. Martin Albrow surveys the criticisms of Weber's concept and offers a defense of Weber in *Bureaucracy*, New York, 1970, pp. 54-66.

[24] Robert K. Merton, "Bureaucratic Structure and Personality," *Social Forces* 18 (May 1940), pp. 560-68. Other works that take similar positions include Alvin W. Gouldner, *Patterns of Industrial Bureaucracy*, Glencoe, Ill., 1955; Peter Blau, *The Dynamics of Bureaucracy*, rev. ed., Chicago, 1963; and Philip Selznick, *TVA and the Grass Roots*, New York, 1966.

bureaucracy as a form of government. What Mill has in mind is the common nineteenth-century contrast between English and Continental forms of government. During most of the century both English and Continental writers agreed that bureaucracy was, in Carlyle's words, "the Continental nuisance." The overbearing power of a bureaucratic state was not thought to be a danger for England.[25] It was not until after the reforms of the English civil service, the most important of which took place in 1870, that observers began to recognize that England was not so immune to the "Continental nuisance" after all.[26]

Because Mill generally treats bureaucracy itself as a form of government, he rarely attends to the dangers of bureaucracy as a part of democratic government. When Mill discusses bureaucracy *in* a democracy, he concentrates on the need for professionalism in the civil service. Since civil servants should not be removed except for the most serious misconduct, they must be appointed with great care in the first place. Appointments should be made by competitive examination, subject to no private or political interest. The examinations are to test candidates' proficiency in the ordinary branches of liberal education—not because such broad competence is necessary in the civil service, but simply because it is an impartial and easily available indication of their general intellectual abilities. Mill also insists on the importance of individual responsibility in administra-

[25] Thomas Carlyle, "The New Downing Street," in *Works*, vol. xx, New York, 1898, p. 143. Cf. J. S. Blackie, "Prussia and the Prussian System," *Westminster Review* 37 (Jan. 1842), pp. 134-37. More generally, see Albrow (pp. 21-32), on whom I rely here. Cf. Mill "Centralisation," p. 324.

[26] See, e.g., Andrew Lang, *Life, Letters and Diaries of Sir Stafford Northcote*, Edinburgh, 1890, vol. II, pp. 219-20 (speech in Edinburgh, 1884).

tion and follows Bentham in denouncing committees or boards as "screens." "What 'the Board' does is the act of nobody; and nobody can be made to answer for it."[27]

Whether treating bureaucracy as a separate form of government or as a part of democratic government, Mill always associates it with the state. Despite his awareness that organization ("the power of combination") was increasing in all spheres of social life, Mill did not face up to the problems of the growth of administrative structures in private associations.[28] That bureaucracy is a pervasive phenomenon in all of modern society is now widely recognized, and controversy centers mainly on whether anything can be done about it.[29] For a long time, the dominant view among students of the subject was that bureaucratization is inevitable in modern societies. This "metaphysical pathos," as one writer describes it, would have been resisted by Mill.[30] Had Mill lived to witness the spread of bureaucratic forms to all

[27] *CRG*, ch. xiv, pp. 252, 265-73; and "Papers Relating to the Re-Organization of the Civil Service," *Parliamentary Papers* 20 (1854-55), pp. 92-98. However, Alan Ryan shows that Mill was also concerned with the educational effects of civil service reform ("Utilitarianism and Bureaucracy: The Views of J. S. Mill," in Gillian Sutherland [ed.], *Studies in the Growth of Nineteenth-Century Government*, London, 1972, pp. 53-55).

[28] "Tocqueville," in *DD*, pp. 93 ff; and *CRG*, ch. i, pp. 12-13. One of the most influential of the early theorists to treat bureaucracy as a general feature of modern society as a whole—Gaetano Mosca—cited Mill as an important inspiration for his own work. He praised mainly the facts reported by "Stuart-Mill" rather than his interpretations (*Teorica dei governi e governo parlamentare*, 2d ed., Turin, 1925, p. 9).

[29] See James Burnham, *The Managerial Revolution*, New York, 1942; Robert Presthus, *The Organizational Society*, New York, 1962; and Michel Crozier, *The Bureaucratic Phenomenon*, Chicago, 1965.

[30] Alvin W. Gouldner, "Metaphysical Pathos and the Theory of Bureaucracy," *American Political Science Review* 49 (June 1955), pp. 496-507.

large associations in society, he would have levelled the same objections against them as he did against the bureaucratic state. Certainly, his theory points in that direction. However important the competence realized by professional administration and hierarchical organization, the values expressed by the principle of participation must be maintained. When bureaucracy begins to overwhelm those values, Mill consistently reaffirms the principle of participation and seeks to restore a balance between participation and competence. Recently, somewhat in the spirit of Mill, several writers have explored ways to mitigate the undemocratic character of bureaucracies.[31]

The second kind of competence—moral competence—is necessary to counter sinister interests. Orthodox utilitarians (including, eventually, Bentham) held that monarchies and aristocracies are particularly prone to sinister interests. The "grand governing law of human nature," James Mill wrote, is that men "desire as much power as will make persons and properties subservient to their pleasures," and that therefore rulers must be checked by a popular assembly to prevent them from tyrannizing citizens.[32] The younger Mill agrees that such abuse of power is a danger and, as we have seen, partly bases his argument for participation on the need to avert it; but he also recognizes that the majority in a democracy are as capable of pursuing sinister interests as any minority in an aristocracy or monarchy are.[33] Ac-

[31] William A. Niskanen, Jr., *Bureaucracy and Representative Government*, Chicago, 1971, pp. 195-201, 213-23; and Alihu Katz and Brenda Danet (eds.), *Bureaucracy and the Public*, New York, 1973.

[32] James Mill, *Essay on Government*, ch. IV, p. 56.

[33] *CRG*, ch. VI, p. 125. Cf. Macaulay, "Mill on Government," pp. 294-95.

cordingly, the orthodox utilitarian theory of democracy must be modified to provide for protection against sinister interests of the majority. These sinister interests are part of the general problem to which Mill elsewhere gives the name "tyranny of the majority."[34]

Educing a theme implicit in Tocqueville's writings, Mill distinguishes two broad kinds of majority tyranny. First, what may be called *political* tyranny of the majority occurs when a majority of the electorate or the legislature enact laws or adopt policies against the general interest, or fail to act against individuals or groups threatening the general interest. Second, *social* tyranny takes place when the majority act through public opinion to impose their own beliefs and values on society.[35]

Mill suggests that political tyranny of the majority may take the form of oppression of a racial, religious, or sectional minority, but the form he discusses in most detail is the violation of the rights of a wealthy minority by a poorer majority. Presumably, he does so because class was, as it is now, the most salient social division in England. That the numerical majority may enact laws weakening the security of property and reducing economic incentives to produce is a real danger because the majority cannot be expected to see that such laws are not in their real interest (especially since the laws may not in fact be), and they are not likely to look out consistently for the interests of future majorities.[36]

Mill's fears of majority tyranny recall those of James Madison, who in the *Federalist Papers* also searches for ways to prevent domination by a majority whose in-

[34] "Tocqueville," in *DD*, pp. 114-17; *Liberty*, ch. I, pp. 13-14; and "Bentham," pp. 107-9.

[35] "Tocqueville," in *DD*, pp. 114-17.

[36] *CRG*, ch. VI, pp. 120-30.

terest is adverse to the "permanent and aggregate interests of the community." Such a majority constitutes one kind of "faction."[37] Mill's definition of political class ("any number of persons who have the same sinister interest") closely parallels Madison's general concept of a faction.[38] The economic basis for the division of society into majority and minority factions figures prominently in Madison's analysis, as it does in Mill's; property, Madison states, is "the most common and durable source of factions."[39] Both theorists count on a balance between conflicting classes or factions as a principal protection against majority tyranny. Madison favors republican government, with its large number of citizens scattered throughout a large territory, because it abets this balance.[40] Similarly, Mill writes that none of the "various sectional interests [ought] to be so powerful as to be capable of prevailing against truth and justice and the other sectional interests combined."[41]

But Mill is not satisfied with a mere balance of factions—and not, as has been suggested, simply because he does not have a large republic at his disposal.[42] Mill recognizes that by itself this balance of competing factions will not consistently yield laws and policies that are in the general interest. Indeed, Mill's argument here contains the seeds of criticisms of Madisonian pluralism that later writers have by now made familiar. Pluralist politics, its critics say, neglects the interests of less powerful groups and militates against public policies (such as conservation of the environment) that are not in the

[37] *The Federalist Papers*, ed. Clinton Rossiter, New York, 1961, "No. 10," pp. 78, 80.
[38] *CRG*, ch. VI, p. 128. [39] *Federalist*, p. 79.
[40] *Federalist*, pp. 82-84. [41] *CRG*, ch. VI, pp. 129-30.
[42] Pitkin, p. 203.

THE PRINCIPLE OF COMPETENCE

immediate interest of any important group.[43] That
pluralist politics in these ways should fail to further the
general interest would not surprise Mill, though in
Representative Government he does not stress, as later
critics do, the social and economic inequalities underlying this failure. From Mill's perspective, what the
pluralist conception of politics omits is political leadership and political education. Without these, citizens
"who act on higher motives, and more comprehensive
and distant views" cannot command sufficient influence
to guide the competing interests (which are often only
apparent interests anyhow) toward a resolution that is
in the general interest.[44] Madison maintained that it is
"vain to say that enlightened statesmen will be able to
adjust . . . clashing interests and render them all subservient to the public good. Enlightened statesmen will
not always be at the helm."[45] It is not that Mill is any
more sanguine about the likelihood of enlightened
statesmanship.[46] He simply insists that a political system
that merely balances competing interests, however necessary, is not sufficient for a democracy striving to realize
the general interest. Rather more than Madison, Mill
looks for institutions to encourage leadership by more
competent citizens and to foster the civic education
of citizens. It is true that Mill's belief in the possibility
of civic education betrays a kind of optimism that Madison, holding the causes of factions to be "sown in the
nature of man," cannot abide.[47] There is in Madison's

---

[43] Henry Kariel, *The Decline of American Pluralism*, Stanford, 1961; Robert Paul Wolff, *The Poverty of Liberalism*, Boston, 1968, pp. 122-61; and William E. Connolly (ed.), *The Bias
of Pluralism*, New York, 1969.

[44] *CRG*, ch. VI, p. 130.   [45] *Federalist*, p. 80.

[46] Cf. "Centralisation," pp. 349-50.

[47] *Federalist*, p. 79.

political theory very little trace of the progressive theory of development that underpins Mill's democratic theory.

Many political scientists now deny that majority tyranny is a serious danger because majorities do not rule. Electoral verdicts often do not represent majority opinion on candidates (let alone on specific issues), and pressure groups representing minorities regularly influence government decisions quite independently of elections even when elections do express majority opinion. The result, Robert Dahl maintains, is "minorities rule," and the problem of majority tyranny takes a back seat to the question of "the extent to which various minorities in a society will frustrate the ambitions of one another with the passive acquiescence or indifference" of the majority.[48]

Mill himself doubts that political tyranny of the majority is a cause for anxiety. This kind of tyranny is not likely to occur in the United States because American society is becoming increasingly middle-class and there is thus "no permanent class to be tyrannized over." Even in England the danger of class legislation by a majority is only temporary. The more enduring political danger stems from "antipathies of religion, political party and race," and these do not take the shape of majority rule in the ordinary sense. Majorities do not often pass laws oppressing minorities; rather, they stand by, in silent sympathy, while the rights of minorities are violated by other minorities.[49]

But for Mill the specter of majority tyranny does not

[48] Robert A. Dahl, *A Preface to Democratic Theory*, Chicago, 1956, pp. 124-34; cf. P.G.J. Pulzer, *Political Representation and Elections in Britain*, rev. ed., London, 1972, pp. 141-42.
[49] "Tocqueville," in *DD*, pp. 115-17.

vanish with the assurance that majorities do not rule. While political majorities rarely tyrannize, social majorities commonly do, and they frustrate the emergence of novel ideas, including those of the competent politician. The spread of mass education, the influence of the mass media, and increasing social mobility combine to create a homogeneous culture that suffocates individuality.

> Protection, therefore, against the tyranny of the magistrate is not enough: there needs protection also against the tyranny of the prevailing opinion and feeling; against the tendency of society to impose, by other means than civil penalties, its own ideas and practices as rules of conduct on those who dissent from them. . . .[50]

According to Mill, it is not democracy, or equality of conditions, that is the principal source of social tyranny, as Tocqueville implies. Tocqueville confuses the effects of equality of conditions with the effects of commercial civilization (the "progress of industry and wealth"). Equality of conditions cannot be a *sufficient* condition of social tyranny, Mill argues, because French Canada enjoys such equality even more than the United States but manifests few of the characteristics of social tyranny. A comparison of Great Britain and the United States shows that equality of conditions cannot be a *necessary* condition of social tyranny either. Of all developed countries, Britain has made the least progress toward equality of conditions, but Britain stands next to America in all the moral and intellectual features (including social tyranny) that Toqueville observed in

[50] *Liberty*, ch. I, p. 13; ch. III, pp. 118-20, 130-33; "Tocqueville," in *DD*, p. 118; and "Civilization," in *DD*, vol. I, pp. 189-91.

America. What Britain and America have in common is a very high level of commercial prosperity, and this similarity may be the cause of the social tyranny and other features Tocqueville found in America.[51] If these comparisons (like those Mill uses to argue for participation) do not quite meet the rigorous standards of proof set forth in the *Logic*, they do indicate that Tocqueville's categories are too crude to generate a completely satisfactory explanation of social tyranny or conformity. But neither does Mill provide more than a sketch of such an explanation. Both Tocqueville and Mill present a better description of social tyranny and its consequences than they do an explanation of its causes.

Mill and Tocqueville were neither the first nor the last observers of American society to be impressed by American conformity. Writings of English travelers to America from 1785 to 1835 virtually all remarked on the "acute sensitiveness to opinion that the average American revealed."[52] Harriet Martineau, who viewed American society at about the same time as Tocqueville but from a different political perspective, noted similar conformist tendencies, as did Max Weber visiting the United States in the early 1900s.[53] By the 1950s conformism had become the prominent theme in the literature of social criticism in the United States.[54] At about

[51] "Tocqueville," in *DD*, pp. 141-45.

[52] Jane L. Mesick, *The English Traveller in America, 1785-1835*, New York, 1922, p. 301.

[53] Harriet Martineau, *Society in America*, New York, 1837, vol. III, pp. 14-15, 17; Max Weber, "Class, Status, Party," in *From Max Weber*, tr. and ed. H. H. Gerth and C. Wright Mills, New York, 1946, p. 188. Cf. James Bryce, *The American Commonwealth*, 2d ed., London, 1891, pp. 331 ff.

[54] Winston White, *Beyond Conformity*, New York, 1961, p. 16. The best known work of this genre is David Riesman's *The Lonely Crowd*, New Haven, 1950, which, despite Riesman's im-

the same time social psychologists began to examine conformity, and their experiments revealed a strong tendency of individuals to conform to the judgments of a group even when the group's judgments were objectively and unambiguously wrong.[55] The few cross-cultural studies that have been conducted seem to support the belief that Americans are more conformist than citizens in some other developed countries.[56]

More recently other social scientists have challenged this conformist picture of American society. They do not question many of the facts brought forward by earlier observers; and they largely ignore the findings of the social psychologists. But they point out that America has always had a large amount of conformity, and some assert that conformity may not only be compatible with liberty and other social values but may be necessary and useful for sustaining these values. Conformity encourages flexibility and stability in a democracy—for example, by facilitating changes in political leadership.[57]

Mill himself did not overlook the value of conformity as a condition for "permanent political society." He

---

plicit denials, has been shown to be very much in the tradition of Tocqueville; see Ralf Dahrendorf, "Democracy Without Liberty: An Essay on the Politics of the Other-Directed Man," in Lipset and Lowenthal, pp. 175-206.

[55] Solomon E. Asch, "Effects of Group Pressure upon the Modification and Distortion of Judgment," in H. Guetzkow (ed.), *Groups, Leadership and Men*, Pittsburgh, 1951, pp. 177-90. Also see Irwin A. Berg and Bernard M. Bass (eds.), *Conformity and Deviation*, New York, 1961.

[56] McClelland, pp. 197-201.

[57] Robert E. Lane and David O. Sears, *Public Opinion*, Englewood Cliffs, N.J., 1964, pp. 83-93; Kluckhohn, p. 187; Lipset, *First New Nation*, pp. 137-39. Cf. David Spitz, *Democracy and the Challenge of Power*, New York, 1958, pp. 46-57.

maintains in his essay on Coleridge that all forms of government, including democracies, require agreement on certain settled principles:

> What, then, enables society to weather these storms [of internal dissension], and pass through turbulent times without any permanent weakening of the securities for peaceable existence? Precisely this— that however important the interests about which men fell out, the conflict did not affect the fundamental principles of the system of social union which happened to exist. . . .

These fundamental principles henceforth are likely to be the principles of individual freedom and political and social equality.[58] A commitment to the form of government itself joins the list in *Representative Government* when Mill lays out the prerequisites for democracy, and the necessity of consensus on basic principles figures importantly in his social statics of democratic society.[59]

Once conformity begins to shade into consensus on fundamental principles, however, the problem is no longer one of too much conformity but of too little—at least with respect to democratic principles. The various empirical studies on consensus reveal a disturbing lack of agreement among citizens on the application of democratic principles to particular cases.[60] Furthermore, the danger that a single political ideology of the majority may be imposed on everyone in society is slight because

[58] "Coleridge," pp. 133-34.

[59] *CRG*, ch. I, pp. 5-9; ch. IV, pp. 70-72. See below, Chapter 4, pp. 141-47.

[60] Herbert McClosky, "Consensus and Ideology in American Politics," *American Political Science Review* 58 (June 1964), pp. 361-82. More generally, see P. H. Partridge, *Consent and Consensus*, London, 1971, pp. 96-138.

few people have anything approaching such an ideology.[61]

To determine whether there is too much or too little conformity in a democracy requires distinctions among various kinds of conformity. It is necessary to know to what opinions individuals are conforming, with whom they share the opinions, and on what basis they accept them. At one extreme we would presumably condemn conformity where an individual accepts undemocratic principles simply because his associates do. At the other extreme we would not object to an individual's accepting the democratic principles of his group where he understands their rationale. In between there are many variants, some of which are problematic. One might, for example, disapprove of the principles to which an individual conforms but admit that his conformity to them has a rational basis that is not simply the result of social pressures. Or one might be satisfied with the principles but troubled by an unthinking acceptance of them. If Mill did not always make such distinctions, neither do most of his modern followers and their critics who write about conformity. It is not then surprising that, despite more than a century of debate about conformity, systematic evidence that would help assess Mill's general complaints about conformity is lacking.

INFLUENCE OF THE COMPETENT

However great may be the danger of a social tyranny of the majority, Mill insists that it is both inevitable and

[61] Philip E. Converse, "The Nature of Belief Systems in Mass Publics," in David E. Apter (ed.), *Ideology and Discontent*, New York, 1964, pp. 206-61. But cf. Norman H. Nie, "Mass Belief Systems Revisited: Political Change and Attitude Structure," *Journal of Politics* 36 (Aug. 1974), pp. 540-91.

right that the majority (the middle class that Mill expected would eventually include most of the working
class) should be the dominant power in a democracy.[62]
How then can the influence of a competent minority
combat the social tyranny of the majority, as the principle of competence demands? *On Liberty*, Mill's chief
work on the nature and prevention of social tyranny, actually suggests very little in the way of means to give
competence its due. If that essay succeeds, it establishes
a distinction between self-regarding actions with which
society should not interfere and other-regarding actions
with which society may interfere.[63] But even the most
generous definition of the self-regarding sphere leaves
an enormous range of activities subject to the legitimate
control of a social or political majority. Indeed, "on
questions of social morality, of duty to others, the opinion of the public, that is, of an overruling majority,
though often wrong, is likely to be still oftener
right. . . ."[64] Although Mill offers some further arguments against government interference, these are not
based on the principle of liberty or on the danger of
majority tyranny. On the contrary, they rest on the same
considerations that bolster the principle of participation
—such as the educative benefits of permitting individuals to make decisions that affect their lives.[65] None of
these considerations provides a social or political basis

[62] "Tocqueville," in *DD*, pp. 98, 156; and *CRG*, ch. VII, p. 132.
[63] A collection that, among other topics, includes discussions
of the controversy over Mill's distinction between self- and other-
regarding actions is Peter Radcliff (ed.), *Limits of Liberty*, Belmont, Calif., 1966.
[64] *Liberty*, ch. IV, p. 150.
[65] *Liberty*, ch. V, pp. 196-201; and *Political Economy*, Bk. V,
ch. XI, §§ 1-6, pp. 936-44.

for the principle of competence. The chief social support for competence Mill at first locates in the agricultural, leisure, and learned classes; but *On Liberty* and *Representative Government* refer merely to the "instructed few," betokening Mill's disillusionment with the aristocracy.[66] The next chapter examines the political institutions that help sustain this social support for the competent to resist "ascendant public opinion," but the nature of the political influence that the competent exert in Mill's representative democracy needs to be considered first.

The political role of the instructed few becomes clearer as Mill elaborates his second general argument for the principle of competence. Just as the educative benefits of participation partly justify the extension of participation, so the educative value of superior competence partly justifies the influence of a competent minority. Here the argument refers primarily to moral competence (a concern for the general interest), though it also includes the ability to reason about the means and ends of broad courses of governmental action. Mill does not think that the instrumental competence that experts and administrators acquire can ever be widely taught.

Civic education does not occur spontaneously. Mill's "school of public spirit" requires teachers as well as scholars:

> [T]he utility of the instruction greatly depends on its bringing inferior minds into contact with superior, a contact which in the ordinary course of life is altogether exceptional, and the want of which

[66] "Tocqueville," in *DD*, pp. 151-55; *Liberty*, ch. III, pp. 119-20; *CRG*, ch. VII, pp. 149-50; and "To John Austin" (April 13, 1847), *Earlier Letters*, in *CW*, vol. XIII, Toronto, 1963, pp. 712-13.

contributes more than anything else to keep the generality of mankind on one level of contented ignorance. . . . A government which [does not show] . . . any one else how to do anything, is like a school in which there is no schoolmaster, but only pupil-teachers who have never themselves been taught.[67]

Mill's description of this process, with its image of political teachers and pupils, sounds elitist, and to some degree it is. But notice that, unlike many contemporary elitist theorists of democracy, Mill does not justify the influence of the competent minority solely on the grounds of its superior ability to govern. The educative goal, which the competent pursue, finds no place in any of the leading elitist democratic theories. The competitive elites who rule in Schumpeter's theory, for example, not only are not expected to educate citizens; they should also not try to engage the interest of citizens in the substance of even major national questions, for by doing so, they would risk uninformed intrusions into the complex process of the making of political decisions.[68]

The instructed few do not literally act like teachers in a classroom. They teach principally by example. Through deliberation in the representative assembly, electoral campaigns, and other public places, they demonstrate how to reason intelligently about the ends of politics.[69] This political discussion should be dialectical

[67] CRG, ch. xv, pp. 282, 294.
[68] Schumpeter, pp. 286-88, 290-96. Also see a sampling of similar views in Henry Kariel (ed.), Frontiers of Democratic Theory, New York, 1970, pp. 31-94.
[69] CRG, ch. xv, pp. 293-94.

—a vigorous encounter of opposing points of view. Parliament, for example, should be "a place where every interest and shade of opinion in the country can have its cause even passionately pleaded, in the face of the government and of all other interests and opinions, can compel them to listen, and either comply, or state clearly why they do not. . . ."[70] Mill's faith in dialetical deliberation as a mode of education grew out of his study of Greek philosophy and his own experience in various discussion groups, such as the London Debating Society.[71] When Mill seeks to transplant such deliberation into the institutions of a large society, he looks to newspapers as the way of "solving the problem of bringing the Democracy of England to vote, like that of Athens, simultaneously in one *agora*. . . ."[72] Yet Mill does not seriously confront the gulf between gathering political knowledge from mass media in this way and engaging in dialectical deliberation. Citizens can take part in such discussion in local government, private associations, and primary groups, but at the national level most people will be at best only passive observers of political deliberations. Nevertheless, Mill is evidently correct in believing that political debate is more enlightening for most people than speeches or statements. In campaign speeches candidates tend to talk past each other and emphasize symbols of consensus, emotional appeals, and generalizations about ends on which everyone can agree. Further, most citizens tend to listen to what they want

[70] *CRG*, ch. v, p. 105. Cf. *Liberty*, ch. II, pp. 31-99.
[71] "Grote's Plato," pp. 271-85; *Inaugural Address*, pp. 354-55; *Autobiography*, ch. IV, pp. 74-78. See Robson, pp. 195-98; and Packe, pp. 53, 67, 69, 70-72, 74, 77, 82-84.
[72] "Tocqueville," in *DD*, 96-97.

to hear and read material in support of what they already believe.[73] When candidates are forced to confront each other in debates, these deficiencies diminish.[74]

The object of dialectical deliberation is of course not solely the education of citizens; the discussion is supposed to influence the decisions that government makes. Since the competent are only a minority, this is often the only way they can influence government. Through deliberations their influence is greater than their numbers: "as a moral power they would count for much more, in virtue of their knowledge, and of the influence it would give them over the rest."[75] Other citizens will in this way defer to the competent, but it is a rather special kind of deference that Mill prescribes.

Four years after the publication of *Representative Government* Bagehot's *The English Constitution* promulgated a sophisticated version of the prevalent notion that the viability of the English political system depends on the "deference of the electors to their betters." The basis of this deference is not intellect but rank and wealth. The mass of the electors "defer to what we may call the *theatrical show* of society . . . a certain pomp of

[73] David E. Butler and Anthony King, *The British General Election of 1964*, London, 1965, pp. 153-55; Butler and Richard Rose, *The British General Election of 1959*, London, 1960, pp. 71-74; Richard Rose, *Influencing Voters: A Study of Campaign Rationality*, New York, 1967, pp. 180-81; and David O. Sears and Jonathan L. Freedman, "Selective Exposure to Information: A Critical View," *Public Opinion Quarterly* 31 (Summer 1967), pp. 194-213.

[74] Stanley Kelley, Jr., "Campaign Debates: Some Facts and Issues," *Public Opinion Quarterly* 26 (Fall 1962), pp. 351-66; and Joseph Trenaman and Denis McQuail, *Television and the Political Image*, London, 1961, pp. 71-74, 90-93. See the discussion and further citations in Thompson, pp. 103-15.

[75] *CRG*, ch. VII, p. 151.

great men." In the second edition of his book in 1872, Bagehot laments that this deference may decline under the impact of electoral reforms and party government.[76]

Mill's idea of deference must be sharply distinguished from Bagehot's. Even when Mill most strongly stresses rule by an elite, he insists that citizens defer to leaders only on rational grounds. It is men's reason that teaches them to respect the authority of still more cultivated minds, and Mill attributes the decline in respect for authority to the incompetence of the men in positions of authority.[77] Bagehot's idea of deference actually comes closer to what Mill calls the theory of dependence, which portrays the relation between the upper and lower classes as one of "affectionate tutelage" on the one side and "respectful grateful deference" on the other. Mill rejects this theory and looks favorably upon the growing reluctance of the working class to be led by the "mere authority and prestige of their superiors."[78]

Earlier Mill mistrusted the ability of most citizens to grasp the reasons for the judgments made by the competent minority. Consequently, he granted the competent almost complete dominance in the process of the formation of political opinions. Political questions should not "be decided by an appeal, *either direct or indirect*, to the judgment or will of an uninstructed mass, whether of gentlemen or clowns; but by the deliberately

[76] Walter Bagehot, *The English Constitution*, ed. R.H.S. Crossman, London, 1963, pp. 247-51, 270-72 (first published as a series of essays in *The Fortnightly* in 1865). Cf. Moisei Ostrogorski, *Democracy and the Organization of Political Parties*, New York, 1964, vol. I, p. 328.

[77] "The Spirit of the Age," *The Examiner* (Jan. 23, 1831), p. 52. The complete series is in F. A. Hayek (ed.), *The Spirit of the Age*, Chicago, 1942.

[78] *Political Economy*, Bk. IV, ch. vii, § 2, p. 764.

formed opinions of a comparatively few, specially educated for the task."[79] He believed that unanimity among
the competent, like that attained by scientists, would
persuade citizens to defer to their authority.[80] Unanimity
was presumably necessary because citizens, not understanding the substance of political questions, could not
make up their minds about which authority to accept
unless the authorities were in agreement. The theme of
unanimity of opinion runs through much of Mill's writing, not only his earlier works. But this unity is a remote
goal—appropriate for a "stage of intellectual advance-
ment which at present seems at an incalculable distance"
—and it has little impact on his theory of government.[81]
For the foreseeable future, diversity is necessary and
desirable, and citizens will have to be able to choose
among members of an instructed minority who will
often disagree.

By the time of *Representative Government* Mill is
ready to dismember the virtual monopoly on political
knowledge and influence that he had conferred upon
the competent minority. Now,

> even supposing the most tried ability and acknowl-
> edged eminence of character in the representative,
> the private opinions of the electors are not to be

[79] "Rationale," pp. 347-48 (italics added).
[80] "Tocqueville" (1835), pp. 111-12n.
[81] *Liberty*, ch. II, pp. 78, 82; ch. III, p. 100; and *Comte*, pp.
325-26. Some commentators have played on this theme of unity
to create an interpretation of Mill as the illiberal founder of a
secular religion to be promulgated by a rational clerisy; see Fitzjames Stephen, esp. pp. 52, 238-41; and Maurice Cowling, *Mill
and Liberalism*, Cambridge, Eng., 1963, pp. 106-61. That this is
a misleading interpretation is shown by Duncan, *Marx and Mill*,
pp. 276-80, and R. J. Halliday, "Some Recent Interpretations of
John Stuart Mill," *Philosophy* 43 (Jan. 1968), pp. 15-16.

placed entirely in abeyance. Deference to mental superiority is not to go the length of . . . abnegation of any personal opinion.[82]

No longer may deference be construed as a "blind submission of dunces to men of knowledge"; it becomes the "intelligent deference of those who know much to those who know still more."[83] Mill therefore comes to expect more of citizens even when they are merely deciding to whom they will defer. "Those who know much" must know quite a lot. An enlightened public must possess not only a "general knowledge of the leading facts of life, both moral and material, but an understanding . . . [of] the principles and rules of sound thinking. . . ."[84] Thus, the influence of the competent derives not from deference to superior status and prestige or to authority simply because it is unanimous, but from well-informed respect for superior knowledge and judgment. And, as we have seen, the competent have a responsibility to help citizens gain the knowledge on which to base such respect.

Patterns of voting in Britain in recent years suggest prima facie that deference to rank and wealth has persisted longer than Mill might have hoped. Whereas only a tenth of the Labour party's support comes from the middle class, about half of the Conservative party's support comes from the working class, and much of this support has been assumed to rest on deference to the superior status of Tory candidates.[85] Probing behind

---

[82] *CRG*, ch. XII, p. 234.   [83] *Comte*, p. 314.
[84] *Inaugural Address*, pp. 344-45.
[85] David Butler and Donald Stokes, *Political Change in Britain*, 2d ed., London, 1974, pp. 183-84. As these authors point out, the difference between the parties' support appears considerably less when we calculate the percentages within classes, instead of within

these voting patterns, however, political scientists have found that relatively little of the Conservative working-class support is deferential in the sense that Bagehot favored and Mill criticized. One study found that only 39 percent of the working-class Tory voters are genuinely deferential; another study put the figure at only 26 percent. Thus, even most workers who vote Conservative do so because they perceive Tory candidates to have superior experience and ability.[86] Although strains of Conservative political attitudes (including deference) still permeate the working class, two studies project a further erosion of deferential attitudes because these attitudes are more common among older than among younger working-class Tory voters.[87] From these trends Butler and Stokes infer that working-class conservatism may be largely the result of the relatively recent rise of the Labour party as a serious alternative for most British voters.[88] Thus, Mill's belief that the old style of deference would disappear may have been only somewhat premature. But however slow the progress toward a more intelligently grounded deference may be, Mill certainly would welcome it.

Although the basis of deference may be evolving in the direction Mill favored, present-day politicians to whom that deference is paid surely do not qualify as the

---

parties: 32 percent of the working-class voters support the Conservative party while 20 percent of middle-class voters choose Labour.

[86] Eric A. Nordlinger, *The Working-Class Tories*, Berkeley and Los Angeles, 1967, calculated from Table I, pp. 67, 81; and Robert T. McKenzie and Allan Silver, *Angels in Marble*, Chicago, 1968, p. 182.

[87] Butler and Stokes, pp. 185-86; and McKenzie and Silver, pp. 183-90. But cf. Nordlinger, pp. 67-68.

[88] Butler and Stokes, pp. 185 ff.

competent leaders Mill envisaged. Mill's competent minority are supposed to perceive and pursue the general interest because they stand above partial and conflicting private interests in society. They are governed by higher considerations than party or pressure group because their loyalty to truth and the general interest is greater than their loyalty to any particular interest. If democratic society for the time being cannot be classless, its competent minority must be.[89] Earlier Mill thought of the competent minority almost exclusively as belonging to the upper classes. The class bias of their backgrounds, if not their beliefs, was undisguised when he wrote in 1835 that "even in the most democratic constitution" political power will remain "mainly in the hands of the rich."[90] But in *Representative Government* the class bias wanes, even in the social background of the competent leadership. The poorer classes, for example, should not be expected to choose an upper-class representative unless they can be sure that he is free "from the class-interests of the rich."[91] If competent leaders eventually arise mostly from the middle class, Mill's pointed critique of middle-class values, especially as they are manifested in conformity and materialism, should dispel any suspicion that he sought a bourgeois ruling class in any usual sense. Although Mill's portrait of the competent politician makes room for the person who has greater practical than theoretical wisdom, his ideal combines both kinds of wisdom—a worldly intellectual without taint of class prejudice.

Since Mill's time the belief that intellectuals, worldly or otherwise, could serve as classless leaders of society

[89] *CRG*, ch. VI, pp. 129-30.   [90] "Rationale," p. 351.
[91] *CRG*, ch. XII, p. 230. Also see "Tocqueville," in *DD*, pp. 95-96; and "To Austin," pp. 712-13. Cf Chapter 3 below, pp. 114-15.

has still found forceful advocates—at least among intellectuals. Mosca expressed this view in almost a pure form: intellectuals comprise the only group that can at least temporarily ignore their private interest and take a detached view of the common good.[92] Karl Mannheim similarly saw the "socially unattached intelligentsia," drawn from the whole range of social classes, as capable of taking a comprehensive and objective view of society.[93] Reviewing the evidence about the role of intellectuals, T. B. Bottomore finds some truth in the assertion that the intelligentsia form a relatively classless group that can better defend more general interests in society. But he notes that the prestige and influence of intellectuals vary greatly from country to country and in different historical periods; they have been much more prominent in politics in France, for example, than in Germany, the United States, or Britain. Moreover, much evidence shows that intellectuals are "influenced very strongly by their social class origins." Although the power of certain types of intellectuals (especially scientists and technicians) has burgeoned in recent years, these groups are ill-equipped to serve as political leaders and civic educators on general political questions because of the specialized nature of their competence.[94] These specialized elites plainly cannot fulfill the functions that Mill assigned to his competent minority, and it

[92] Mosca, *Teorica*, p. 142.
[93] Karl Mannheim, *Ideology and Utopia*, tr. Louis Wirth and Edward Shils, London, 1963, pp. 136 ff.
[94] T. B. Bottomore, *Elites and Society*, London, 1964, pp. 66-71. Cf. Raymond Aron, *The Opium of the Intellectuals*, tr. Terence Kilmartin, London, 1957; Henry M. MacDonald (ed.), *The Intellectual in Politics*, Austin, Texas, 1966; Philip Rieff (ed.), *On Intellectuals*, New York, 1969; and Edward Shils, *The Intellectuals and the Powers and Other Essays*, Chicago, 1972.

is hard to locate in most modern democracies any politically influential group that would do so.

None of this recent analysis detracts from Mill's claim that a competent minority are necessary in a democracy. Democracies without them suffer from many of the shortcomings that Mill alleged their absence would in fact encourage; and nothing has disproved Mill's contention that democracies with an influential competent minority would help overcome some of these failings. What is in doubt is how a competent minority could actually acquire the influence that Mill expected them to exercise. His theory of development, which is meant to explain how the competent could become more influential in the future, is questionable. And the theory of government, which is supposed to provide competent leaders with some means of exercising influence in the meantime, grants them a more constricted role than one would expect in light of Mill's general statements about the great importance of competence. These statements turn out to be an unreliable indicator of the role of the competent minority in the political institutions depicted in *Representative Government*, though they are a guide that many commentators unhesitatingly follow. Even those commentators who recognize the elements in Mill's thought that subvert elite rule nevertheless declare that the competent minority are to be "dominant" in the institutions proposed in *Representative Government*.[95] However, an examination of those institutions (as the next chapter shows) does not support this claim. Tempered by the principle of participation, the institutions

[95] Duncan, *Marx and Mill*, p. 259; cf. Pateman, pp. 32, 33. Duncan seems to qualify this claim with the phrase "if possible," though it is unclear what import the qualification is supposed to convey.

of representative government formally give the competent minority only slightly more political power than that to which their numbers would entitle them anyway, never permitting them to outvote the numerical majority in elections or in the legislature. The competent must finally rely on rational deliberation, which will be effective insofar as they seek to educate citizens.

We have seen that Mill justifies the principle that the more competent should have as much influence as possible, first, in moral theory by invoking his doctrine of higher pleasures and, second, in political theory by showing that competence is necessary to protect against ignorance and sinister interests (especially majority tyranny) both in the government and in the citizenry. The principle is also based on Mill's belief that civic education requires competent leadership. Consequently, the deference that Mill hopes citizens will pay to the instructed few must be consistent with the educational aims of his theory. Still to be considered are the political means by which the competent exercise influence in a democracy and the way in which that influence can in practice be combined with the demands of the principle of participation.

3

The Theory of Government

Unless all citizens are equally and highly competent, the principles of participation and competence may conflict. If participation becomes more extensive, the influence of the competent minority may decrease; or if the influence of the competent remains strong, participation may not be very extensive. But Mill refuses to reject either principle. He in effect criticizes earlier theorists for failing to recognize that both these principles have an essential role in political theory. Plato's strength, Mill writes, is his belief that government requires special skill or competence, but his weakness is his refusal to recognize the legitimacy of giving political power to all citizens; he mistakenly assumes that rulers are infallible, or that citizens are utterly incompetent.[1] Benthamites, in contrast, yield too much to the demand for extensive participation; they neglect to moderate the power of the majority with some "deference to the superiority of cultivated intelligence."[2] Mill's own theory of government combines the strengths of both of these perspectives, in accord with his general habit of synthesizing the "one-eyed" insights of his predecessors.

Mill does not intend to resolve fully the conflict between the principles of participation and competence, since a tension between the two principles is an essential

[1] "Grote's Plato," pp. 324-25.
[2] "Bentham," p. 108.

feature of his theory of government. The theory defines the nature of that tension, sets limits to its resolution, and suggests practical ways in which a resolution might be approximated. The resolution, or the synthesis of the principles, takes place only in practical political life through political institutions or processes, which are designed to express at the same time the value of both participation and competence. The theory of government indicates the form these institutions should take and provides standards by which they can be judged, but it does not determine the precise balance between the principles.

A MIXED THEORY OF DEMOCRATIC GOVERNMENT

Walter Bagehot set forth two theories of British government—both erroneous, in his view—that he believed held sway in nineteenth-century England. One was the doctrine of the separation of powers, according to which the legislative, executive, and judicial powers are each entrusted to separate persons or groups of persons who may not encroach upon each other's authority. The other was the theory of mixed or balanced government, which holds that the monarchical, aristocratic, and democratic elements in the constitution should each share in the supreme sovereignty.[3]

Mill subscribes to neither of these two doctrines in their pure form. Although he fails to stress, as Bagehot does, the increasing importance of the Cabinet as the "connecting link" between the executive and legislature,

---

[3] Bagehot, pp. 59-60. M.J.C. Vile shows that Bagehot's account of the "accepted" theories is misleading; most serious writers adopted more subtle theories, some much like Mill's (*Constitutionalism and the Separation of Powers*, Oxford, 1967, pp. 212-23).

Mill does not accept the doctrine of the separation of powers.[4] Not only does he recognize the growing influence of the executive in the legislative process, but he also favors an even greater role for the executive in that process, as we shall see.

Mill's attitude toward the theory of mixed government is more complex. A classic formulation of that theory is in Aristotle's *Politics,* a work Mill dismisses as a "philosophic consecration of existing facts," especially of those facts that promote stability rather than improvement. Aristotle, the "moderate aristocratical politician," leaves no room for a progressive theory of development.[5] More specifically, Aristotle's mixed government (*politeia*) is his second-best regime, the best constitution for most cities and most of mankind, while Mill's representative government is under favorable conditions the "ideal type of a perfect government." Furthermore, Aristotle's mixed government combines two forms of government in one so that the resulting mixture can be described indifferently as either; *politeia* may be called either a democracy or an oligarchy.[6] Mill doubts that any such perfect balance could ever be attained. The "scales never hang exactly even" because the constitution must favor the strongest power in society, and in modern societies like Britain and the United States this power is the democratic majority. Mill's constitution is thus fundamentally democratic.[7]

[4] Cf. R.H.S. Crossman, "Introduction," in Bagehot, pp. 8-9.

[5] "Grote's Aristotle," in *DD*, vol. v, p. 207.

[6] *Politics*, Bk. IV, 1295.a25-31, pp. 326-27; 1294.b15-20, pp. 321-22. Aristotle does not reconcile (a) his account of *politeia* as a mixture of oligarchy and democracy; and (b) his classification of *politeia* as a good form of government, and democracy and oligarchy as bad forms.

[7] *CRG*, ch. VI, pp. 87-89; ch. VII, p. 132.

To reject a mixed or balanced constitution is not necessarily to repudiate the need for checks on the sovereign power. No theorist heaped more scorn on the idea of mixed government than Bentham did.[8] Yet Bentham came to believe that checks on the supreme power are necessary, and he admired this feature of the American constitution.[9] While Mill also favors checks, he insists that they be located within the democratic elements of the constitution, not in separate, countervailing institutions. Mill's view of a second chamber, which proponents of mixed government often saw as a principal check on democratic power, illustrates his reasons for insisting on this point. The influence of a second chamber like the House of Lords, Mill argues, depends on its social support, and in an increasingly democratic society an aristocratic chamber will command less and less respect.[10] Mill's prognosis has turned out to be correct, as second chambers have generally ceased to be an effective check on democratic majorities.[11] If there is to be a second chamber at all, Mill thinks, it should take the form of a Chamber of Statesmen, composed of the most competent persons who have held important political office. It would not try to veto legislation but would guide it "in the path of prog-

[8] Bentham, *A Fragment on Government,* ed. Wilfred Harrison, Oxford, 1960, chs. III-IV, pp. 69-103; and *The Book of Fallacies,* in *Works,* vol. II, pp. 445-47.

[9] Bentham, *The Elements of the Art of Packing,* in *Works,* vol. V, pp. 69-70; and *Constitutional Code,* in *Works,* vol. IX, pp. 123-24. Mill tends to neglect this aspect of Bentham's theory.

[10] *CRG,* ch. XIII, pp. 241-43. Cf. Vile, pp. 33-34.

[11] John C. Adams, *The Quest for Democratic Law,* New York, 1970, pp. 132-33; and K. C. Wheare, *Legislatures,* London, 1963, pp. 197-218.

ress."[12] The "really moderating power in a democratic constitution, must act in and through the democratic House" and presumably the electoral processes in which its members are chosen.[13]

Despite Mill's basic divergences from the traditional theory of mixed government, the structure of his own theory is *in form* rather like Aristotle's version of that theory. As Aristotle mixes the competing claims of oligarchy and democracy, so Mill combines the conflicting principles of competence and participation. The balance both theorists wish to strike between the competing principles is determined not theoretically but practically through political processes and institutions. Aristotle's theory apportions the influence of each kind of claim in accordance with its contribution to the common good (for Mill, the criterion is general utility).[14] When Aristotle actually tries to reconcile competing claims, he simply proposes a set of political institutions, each of which simultaneously incorporates equal elements of oligarchic and democratic principles. For example, the method of choosing magistrates in a *politeia* combines the oligarchic rule of election (rather than lot) and the democratic rule of free-birth suffrage (rather than a property qualification).[15] Formally in the same way, Mill combines elements of the principles of participation and competence in *each* major institution or process of a democracy. The

[12] *CRG*, ch. xiii, p. 243. Mill approves of the U.S. Senate because he believes it attracts more competent members (ch. xvii, pp. 503-4). But Bentham included the Senate in his general attack on second chambers; see "Anti-Senatica," *Smith College Studies in History* 11 (July 1926), pp. 209-67.

[13] *CRG*, ch. xiii, p. 242.

[14] *Politics*, Bk. iii, 1280.a9 – 1284.a3, pp. 211-41.

[15] *Politics*, Bk. iv, 1294.a30 – 1294.b14, pp. 319-21.

parallel between the two theories of course does not extend to the content of all the key terms. The claims of Aristotle's oligarchy, for example, rest on wealth, which for Mill is not the basis of competence.[16] And even though Aristotle justifies democracy with some arguments akin to Mill's, Aristotle does not have in mind modern representative democracy.[17] But while the content of Mill's theory of government departs from that of traditional mixed theories, its formal structure remains that of a mixed theory of democratic government.

THE ELECTORAL PROCESS

The principle of participation, in Mill's view, implies universal suffrage. The reasons Mill gives for not excluding any portion of the citizens from a voice in representation exactly parallel the arguments he presents for extensive participation.[18] None of the arguments assumes that the franchise is a right each citizen may use as he pleases; rather, the arguments are supposed to show that granting the franchise to all citizens will in one way or another further general utility and thus make everyone better off. The reason that voting cannot be a right in this sense is that it is a "power over others," and no one can have a right to such power except as it is exercised in the general interest. Mill thus prefers to treat voting as a trust or duty.[19]

[16] *Politics*, Bk. IV, 1294.a23-8, p. 319.
[17] *Politics*, Bk. III, 1281.b – 1282.a24, pp. 219-27; Bk. IV, 1294.b8-15, pp. 320-21.
[18] *CRG*, ch. VIII, pp. 164-68.
[19] *CRG*, ch. X, pp. 198-201; and *Comte*, p. 304. In *CRG* (ch. VIII, p. 187) and in *Subjection of Women* (ch. III, pp. 96-97), Mill does refer to a "right" to vote, but presumably even here he assumes that rights are reducible to utility and thus subject to

Mill's justification of suffrage contrasts with that which social contract theory offers. The best contemporary version of contract theory justifies an equal right to vote on grounds of justice, not general utility. In an original position, mutually disinterested individuals, who do not know such facts as their social position or conception of the good, would adopt principles of justice that guarantee everyone basic liberties including the right to equal participation. These basic liberties could not be sacrificed or limited for the sake of an increase in general utility (as at least the right to vote could be in Mill's theory). The preservation of basic liberties, which everyone, whatever his goals, needs to control his prospects in life, are more important than any gain in material welfare above a minimal level.[20] Since Mill in his conception of utility assigns a high priority to liberty (as well as to participation), the difference between the practical implications of his theory and those of social contract theory may be slight under most actual conditions, but the difference in the reasoning or justification remains significant.

One consequence of Mill's justification of suffrage is that a voter must "consider the interest of the public, not his private advantage, and give his vote to the best of his judgment, exactly as he would be bound to do if he were the sole voter, and the election depended upon him alone."[21] Mill conceives of this as an ideal, and he is quite prepared to permit apparent interests, which may contradict the general interest, to have a role in the political process. They should have a role, not as a

---

restrictions imposed for the sake of the general interest (see *Utilitarianism*, ch. v, pp. 250, 258).

[20] Rawls, pp. 221-22, 541-48.

[21] *CRG*, ch. x, p. 201.

matter of right, but as a precaution against their being ignored when they do happen to coincide with the general interest, and as a means of their being modified, through the educative effects of participation, so that they may eventually fall more into line with the general interest.

A second, now rather curious, consequence of Mill's rationale for suffrage is his opposition to the secret ballot. The ballot was a chief goal of the Philosophic Radicals and of Mill himself for some time.[22] But by 1859 Mill felt that the dangers of intimidation and coercion of voters, which the secret ballot was supposed to discourage, had abated. The greater danger had become that voters in the cloak of secrecy would forget that voting is a *public* trust.[23] Modern democracies generally have not adopted Mill's open ballot no doubt because they reasonably feel that secret voting is still required to prevent intimidation and the selling of votes. The secret ballot may also help reduce conformity to opinions of one's peers—an advantage that Mill overlooked.[24]

Mill's theory dilutes universal suffrage by denying the right to vote to persons who cannot read, write, or do simple arithmetic, who pay no taxes, or who receive welfare (parish relief). None of these exclusions is based on the principle of competence (though Mill refers to

[22] "Parliamentary Proceedings of the Session," *London Review* 1 (July 1835), pp. 514-17. Cf. Gerald McNiece, "Shelley, John Stuart Mill and the Secret Ballot," *Mill News Letter* 8 (Spring 1973), pp. 2-7.

[23] *Thoughts on Parliamentary Reform*, in *DD*, vol. iv, pp. 36-48 (quoted in *CRG*, ch. x, pp. 203-11). Even James Mill had conceded that a developed democracy such as the United States did not need a secret ballot ("The Ballot," *Westminster Review* 13 [July 1830], p. 26).

[24] On the development of the secret ballot, see Stein Rokkan, *Citizens, Elections, Parties*, New York, 1970, pp. 152-55.

that idea in defending the first exclusion). The rationale for all of the exclusions evidently is the same as that which underlies the protective argument for participation: a "power of control" (the vote) must be in the hands of only those who have an interest in its beneficial exercise. The excluded groups have not demonstrated even the most minimal interest in taking care of themselves, let alone an interest in the general good. Mill regards all three of the exclusions as temporary, however, and insists that the government is obliged to give all individuals the opportunity to overcome them.[25] In *Representative Government* Mill sometimes assumes that individuals can, solely by their own efforts, rise out of the poverty that disqualifies them from voting.[26] But the year after the publication of the book, he maintains that the government must compensate for any natural inequalities, which, by their "crushing and dispiriting" unfairness, discourage the poor from improving their circumstances. And in "Chapters on Socialism," published posthumously, he stresses that effort and skill are not sufficient for overcoming poverty: "Next to birth, the chief cause of success in life is accident and opportunity."[27]

One method Mill proposes for implementing the principle of competence in the electoral process is plural voting. On this proposal, citizens who are more competent are entitled to one (or more) extra votes. His argument for the proposal is the same as the general argu-

[25] *CRG*, ch. VIII, pp. 168-72.
[26] *CRG*, ch. VIII, p. 173; but cf. pp. 175-76.
[27] "Centralisation," p. 334; and "Chapters on Socialism," in *CW*, Toronto, 1967, vol. V, pp. 714-15. Some earlier suggestions of this general idea are in *Utilitarianism*, ch. II, p. 216; and *Subjection of Women*, esp. ch. III, pp. 103-6, and ch. IV, pp. 153-54.

ment for competence we examined in Chapter 2.[28] By the time Mill wrote *Representative Government*, however, his enthusiasm for plural voting was waning, partly because of the difficulty of finding a satisfactory criterion for determining who is competent enough to receive the extra votes. In the absence of a national system of education, the least unsatisfactory criterion, Mill thinks, is occupation; higher-status jobs generally require more intelligence. But Mill does not finally endorse even this criterion because it is open to many objections; he himself states one earlier in the same paragraph when presenting the criterion: "accident has so much more to do than merit with enabling men to rise in the world."[29] Furthermore, Mill considerably weakens the political impact that plural voting could have by insisting that those who receive the extra votes, or the class to which they mainly belong, must not be able to outvote the rest of the community.[30]

Mill would still favor plural voting because of its favorable influence on the *"spirit* of the institutions of a country," even if it had no direct effect on the outcome of any election. It enshrines the principle of competence in the constitution, thereby declaring that "ignorance [is not] entitled to as much political power as knowledge."[31] However, the trouble with such spiritual effects is that they depend so much on the traditional connotations of the institution in question. Since plural voting was traditionally associated with the protection

[28] *CRG*, ch. VIII, pp. 173-78.

[29] *CRG*, ch VIII, p. 176.

[30] *CRG*, ch. VIII, p. 178. A few years earlier he seemed to imply that plural voting could prevent the minority from always being outvoted by the majority (*Thoughts on Parliamentary Reform*, p. 27).

[31] *CRG*, ch. VIII, p. 182; ch. XII, pp. 231-32.

of property interests, the spirit that it was likely to impart was just the opposite of what Mill intended. Later recognizing this unintended consequence, Mill notes that most proponents of schemes like plural voting are more interested in fortifying property than in venerating superior intelligence. With a system of national education by which various levels of political competence might be certified, Mill feels that plural voting could have the spiritual effects he hopes for. But with such a system of education, he concludes, plural voting would perhaps not be needed at all.[32]

Although political writers still propose plural voting from time to time, modern democracies have generally rejected the idea, except in a few municipal elections on certain issues.[33] The British practice of granting an extra vote to university graduates to choose an M.P., which was abolished in 1948, is sometimes identified with Mill's proposal.[34] But in fact Mill objected to any scheme that would set up a separate constituency for the instructed minority. It would, he believed, exacerbate class divisions, bring education into disrespect, and not encourage the selection of competent persons anyhow. The experience of learned societies shows that intellectual men seldom give their vote to the most intellectual among their members.[35]

One reason that Mill did not despair of the inability of plural voting to realize the principle of competence in elections is that he found what he considered to be a

[32] *Autobiography*, ch. VII, pp. 153-54. This section was probably written in 1869-70.

[33] A recent advocate is Joseph Farkas, "One Man, 1/4 Vote," *New York Times*, March 29, 1974, p. 22.

[34] Brian Barry, *The Liberal Theory of Justice*, Oxford, 1973, p. 146.

[35] *Thoughts on Parliamentary Reform*, pp. 27-28n.

better way of achieving the same goal: Thomas Hare's system of Personal Representation (now commonly called the system of the single-transferable vote).[36] According to Hare's proposal, voters indicate on their ballots their order of preferences for candidates (first, second, third choice, and so on). Any candidate who receives the required quota when the first-place preferences are counted is elected. (The quota is simply the number of valid ballots cast divided by the number of seats to be filled—658 in 1865.)[37] If any candidate receives more than the quota, his surplus is distributed to the candidates who appear as the second choice on the surplus ballots.[38] This process of redistribution continues through the third and lower choices until 658 candidates reach the quota and are elected.[39] Votes cast

[36] CRG, ch. VII, pp. 139-62; and Thomas Hare, *The Election of Representatives: Parliamentary and Municipal*, London, 1859. Mill used this edition, but the citations below are to the third edition (London, 1865).

[37] Hare eventually modified the quota (pp. 305-7), accepting Henry Droop's formula, which is closer to modern practice: [votes ÷ (seats + 1)] + 1. See Droop, "On the Political and Social Effects of Different Methods of Electing Representatives," *Papers Read Before the Juridical Society*, London, 1871, vol. III, p. 471.

[38] To determine which ballots are redistributed and which remain to make up the winning candidate's quota, Hare suggests either a very complicated set of rules or a random procedure (pp. ix, 161). In the best modern systems, the candidates listed next on *all* of the ballots cast for the candidates who reach their quota (or who are eliminated) receive a proportionate share of the surplus.

[39] In the event that some of the seats are still unfilled after this redistribution, the candidates who have the highest rankings on the largest number of unassigned ballots are declared elected, even though they do not have the quota. In his first edition Hare proposes a different method at this stage in the process: the

for a candidate in his own local constituency are counted first; votes from other constituencies are counted only if he does not reach the quota with votes from his own constituency. Although local constituencies could thus still have their own candidate(s), national constituencies would now be able to elect an M.P. Because of this possibility, Mill thought that the problem of inequalities in the size of electoral districts would not be very serious.[40]

Upon reading the first edition of Hare's book in 1859, Mill wrote to the author:

> You appear to me to have exactly, and for the first time, solved the difficulty of popular representation; and by doing so, to have raised up the cloud of gloom and uncertainty which hung over the futurity of representative government and therefore of civilization. That you are right in theory I never could have doubted, and as to practice, having begun with a great natural distrust of what seemed a very complicated set of arrangements, I ended by being convinced that the plan is workable. . . .[41]

---

candidates with the lowest number of votes are eliminated, one by one, and their ballots redistributed until all the seats are filled by persons who have reached the quota. This method comes closer to the modern "elimination" procedure (see Enid Lakeman, *How Democracies Vote*, 3d ed., London, 1970, pp. 112-17). Hare abandoned it in response to objections from Mill (among others), who thought it created a bias in favor of party lists and against independent candidates (Hare, pp. 184-85, 189-92; Mill, *CRG*, ch. VII, p. 158).

[40] Cf. "Recent Writers," p. 91.

[41] March 3, 1859, *Later Letters*, in *CW*, Toronto, 1972, vol. XV, pp. 598-99. Mill first publicly advocated Hare's system in April 1859 in "Recent Writers," pp. 78-100.

Mill's enthusiasm for Hare's proposal never slackened, and in 1867 in the House of Commons he advocated its adoption.[42]

For Mill, the appeal of Personal Representation was that it could satisfy both his principle of participation and his principle of competence in a single institution at the same time. It is sometimes assumed that Mill supported the Hare plan essentially to strengthen the influence of the elite.[43] Undoubtedly, this was an important advantage of the plan in Mill's eyes. Distinguished persons, who might not win a majority in any local constituency, would be more likely to secure the required quota if they had the electorate of the whole nation to draw upon. Their presence in Parliament would improve the quality of the deliberations, and though they could easily be outvoted, they would have great "moral influence" over the other representatives. Moreover, the majority parties, faced with competition from these distinguished national candidates, would have a greater incentive to seek more competent persons to run under the party banner.[44]

But the advantages for the principle of competence are only part of Mill's case for Personal Representation. The protection of interests, called for by the principle of participation, is better realized by Hare's system than

[42] *Personal Representation*, London, 1867. Besides Mill's speech of May 29, 1867, this contains Robert Lytton's report on the Danish electoral system to which Mill refers in later editions of *CRG*, ch. VII, pp. 161-62n. Also see *Autobiography*, ch. VII, pp. 153-54.

[43] E.g., Paul B. Kern, "Universal Suffrage Without Democracy: Thomas Hare and J. S. Mill," *Review of Politics* 34 (July 1972), p. 318. Cf. F. L. van Holthoon, *The Road to Utopia*, Assen, 1971, p. 121.

[44] *CRG*, ch. VII, pp. 144-52.

by a majoritarian system with single-member districts. The latter system effectively silences those citizens who happen to be in the minority in a particular constituency. This, Mill maintains, is not true democracy— "government of the whole people by the whole people, equally represented." Not merely the instructed minority, but *"every* or *any* section" of the electorate must be represented proportionately.[45] Hare's system makes participation more meaningful in another way as well, according to Mill. Since every M.P. would be the representative of a unanimous constituency, the "tie between the elector and the representative" would be vastly strengthened. Virtually every citizen would have a representative who specifically represented his or her interests or enjoyed his or her trust.[46] Furthermore, this stronger relation between voters and their representatives could enhance the educative value of participation by giving citizens a greater sense of influence over the outcome of the elections and the behavior of their representatives.[47] (A point Mill does not note is that the tie between voters and representatives would not be so strong in Hare's system unless voting were public, which Mill of course favors.) Finally, the majoritarian electoral system may strip even a real majority of the electorate of their rightful control of government. If Parliament is composed of members who have been elected by narrow majorities in each constituency, any bill that passes by a

[45] *CRG,* ch. VII, pp. 131-33 (italics added). Fairer representation of all minorities that voters see as significant is a chief advantage cited by modern proponents of the single-transferable vote (Lakeman, pp. 128-30; Rokkan, p. 157).

[46] *CRG,* ch. VII, pp. 142-43; cf. Lakeman, pp. 141-42.

[47] Hare, pp. xx-xxv. Cf. W.J.M. Mackenzie, *Free Elections,* New York, 1958, pp. 73-74.

bare majority could easily be against the will of a real majority in the country.[48] Thus, Personal Representation, which would not have this consequence, is required by a "radical" creed that cares for the interests of the majority, as well as by a "conservative" creed that respects the interests of the propertied and the educated.[49]

Mill's argument for Personal Representation, some have claimed, is not consistent with his argument for plural voting.[50] The former is desirable (in part) because it ensures that citizens will be represented according to their numerical strength; this equal representation is the "principle of democracy, which professes equality as its very root and foundation."[51] But Mill's argument for plural voting denies that everyone should have an equal vote.[52]

One commentator attempts to overcome this inconsistency by creating a distinction between Mill's aim of securing true rather than false democracy and his aim of establishing ideal representative government rather than democracy, however "true." On this interpretation, plural voting, which supports ideal representative government, takes precedence over Hare's system, which supports merely a true democracy, because even true democracy "in the last resort fails by Mill's standards."[53] The trouble with this interpretation is, first, that Mill

[48] *CRG*, ch. VII, pp. 133-34; "To Thomas Hare," June 17, 1859, *Later Letters*, in *CW*, vol. xv, p. 626. Cf. Lakeman, pp. 39-42.
[49] *Personal Representation*, p. 15; and *CRG*, Preface, pp. v-vi.
[50] Anschutz, p. 45n.
[51] *CRG*, ch. VII, p. 132; and *Personal Representation*, p. 14.
[52] *CRG*, ch. VIII, pp. 173-74.
[53] Burns (Oct. 1957), pp. 293-94.

never distinguishes true democracy from ideal representative government; the only explicit distinction is between true and false democracy.[54] Second, Mill never rejects true democracy, as he defines it; on the contrary, the rationale for the principle of participation that he repeatedly affirms strongly implies true democracy. Finally, Mill's growing reservations about plural voting—not only in existing social conditions but also in future ones—strongly suggest that, if for the sake of consistency he were forced to choose between the two, he would opt for Hare's system. Mill himself indicates such a preference: "I should not despair of the operation even of equal and universal suffrage, if made real by . . . Mr. Hare's principle."[55]

Because in *Representative Government* Mill does not actually choose between Personal Representation and plural voting, the inconsistency persists. It is not, however, so fundamental as it may appear, since it does not reflect a contradiction in his basic idea of equality. Rather, it is a consequence of his attempt to apply egalitarian and inegalitarian standards to the same act—voting. Mill could maintain, as he does much of the time, that all citizens should have equal *votes*, but that they should voluntarily grant more competent individuals greater or unequal *influence* in political deliberations. In this way the strict contradiction would dissolve, though the tension between equal voting (implied by the principle of participation) and unequal influence (implied by competence) would remain, to be

[54] Cf. *CRG*, ch. VII, pp. 131-32; ch. VIII, pp. 163, 177.
[55] *CRG*, ch. VIII, p. 181; and "To Charles A. Cummings," Feb. 23, 1863, *Later Letters*, in *CW*, vol. xv, p. 843.

worked out in practice with the aid of Personal Representation.[56]

Hare's system has not been widely adopted in modern democracies. By the early part of this century, many European democracies had instituted a form of proportional representation with party lists (a system that generally gives less scope to individual preference than Hare's system does). Only Ireland now uses Hare's system (slightly modified) in national elections.[57] Britain has seen several serious attempts to win parliamentary approval for similar systems come to little.[58] Why has a system that Mill counted "among the very greatest improvements in the theory and practice of government" failed to carry the day? Not, as some commentators imply, because Mill was simply wrong about the practical effects of the system.[59] Where it has been tried, Hare's method has worked much as Mill anticipated. Compared to majority or plurality systems, it tends to allocate seats more proportionately and less often denies representation to smaller groups and parties.[60] There is some slight

[56] In *Utilitarianism* Mill's commitment to equality is similarly qualified: Bentham's dictum, "everybody is to count for one, and nobody for more than one," must make the "proper allowance . . . for kind," i.e., higher pleasures or superior competence (ch. v, pp. 257-58).

[57] See Rokkan, pp. 158-61; and J.F.S. Ross, *The Irish Election System*, London, 1959. The system operates in Tasmania, Malta, New South Wales, Australian Senatorial elections, in a number of cities in the United States and Canada, and within various English and American universities.

[58] See David E. Butler, *The Electoral System in Britain since 1918*, 2d ed., Oxford, 1963, pp. 38-48, 58-72.

[59] E.g., Anschutz, pp. 44-45; and Annan, p. 228.

[60] Lakeman, pp. 215-50; Douglas W. Rae, *The Political Consequences of Electoral Laws*, New Haven, 1967, pp. 96-98, 110-11. Rae's findings do not distinguish the Irish system from other PR systems.

evidence that the system increases political participation, as Mill hoped, and (even more speculatively) that it improves the chances of competent candidates in elections.[61]

Objections that Mill and Hare tried to put to rest continue to bedevil proponents of the system. Voters and politicians still resist it no doubt partly because of its complexity, though only electoral officials need to understand its technical details.[62] The ordering of preferences that the system encourages requires more sophisticated voting than merely registering a party preference, which many voters now tend to do.[63] Mill felt the force of a second objection—that the system would destroy the "local character of representation"—enough to suggest a modification to strengthen the influence of localities.[64] Even in its original form, Hare's scheme retains some bias in favor of localities, but since even where the system has been used the provision for national constituencies has not been adopted, what the effect would be on local representation remains uncertain. A third common objection has been that the system gives undue influence to larger parties, which by distributing preference lists to all of their supporters could swamp the smaller parties and the independent

[61] Lakeman, pp. 151-52, 219-20, 243-44.

[62] See *CRG*, ch. vii, pp. 160-1; Hare, pp. vii-xii; and Millicent Fawcett, "Proportional Representation and Hare's Scheme Explained," in Henry and Millicent Fawcett, *Essays and Lectures*, London, 1872, p. 352.

[63] Rae, p. 128; and Campbell et al., pp. 227-65.

[64] *Personal Representation*, p. 10. In *CRG* (p. 152) he does not concede anything to this objection. Cf. Hare, pp. xii-xv; Fawcett, pp. 361-62; and Droop, pp. 485-86, 506-7. Modern commentators perpetuate the mistaken idea that Hare (or Mill) eliminated geographical representation (e.g., Birch, *Representation*, London, 1971, p. 89, and Mackenzie, p. 72).

candidates.[65] Mill conceded this possibility, but pointed out (correctly, it now seems) that the effect would be much less serious under proportional representation than under a majoritarian system.[66]

Mill never confronted the objection most frequently urged by modern critics of various forms of proportional representation, namely, that they undermine stable and effective government by fragmenting party systems and creating minority governments.[67] Although an electoral system is neither a necessary nor a sufficient condition for these effects, there is a strong association between proportional representation and multiparty systems, on the one hand, and majority or plurality systems and two-party systems, on the other.[68] Further, David Butler calculates that if Britain had adopted proportional representation, only two out of the ten elections from 1922 to 1959 would have produced strong majority governments, though (as he admits) people might have voted differently had proportional representation existed.[69] However, Ireland has managed to elect majority governments most of the time. And even if proportional representation does tend to fragment the party system, it is by no means obvious that this in itself prevents stable or effective government. Under many conditions, proportional representation discourages the frequent calling of elections, encourages compromises that take

[65] See, e.g., Bagehot, pp. 166-67.

[66] *CRG*, ch. vii, pp. 156-58; Hare, pp. xv-xvii; and Rae, pp. 88-91.

[67] The most vehement critic is Ferdinand A. Hermens, *Democracy or Anarchy?*, South Bend, Ind., 1941. Cf. Maurice Duverger, *Political Parties*, tr. Barbara and Robert North, New York, 1963, pp. 245-55, 304, 325; and Helmut Unkelbach, *Grundlägen der Wahlsystematik*, Göttingen, 1956.

[68] Rae, pp. 92-96.

[69] Butler, pp. 189-92.

place more often between parties openly in parliament than secretly within party caucuses, and maintains continuity in the legislature better than majority systems that exaggerate changes in the relative electoral strengths of parties.[70] In any case, Mill had no great fondness for the two-party system, as we shall see, since he felt that it limited citizens' choices and stifled political diversity.[71] This was probably a principal reason why the objection that Hare's system might weaken the two-party system did not disturb Mill.

In his enthusiasm for Hare's system, Mill sometimes writes as if electoral engineering could solve all the problems of democratic government. Leslie Stephen points out that in those moods Mill's "faith in a bit of mechanism of 'human contrivance' becomes sublime." Anticipating many modern critics of institutional reform, Stephen observes that political power does not depend primarily on such devices as electoral systems but on the various social, economic, and cultural conditions in society.[72] But Mill himself, in more sober moods, rejects the "analogy of mechanical contrivances" in political reform and strongly insists that many other requisites must be combined with an institutional reform if it is to accomplish its purpose.[73]

Nevertheless, institutions such as electoral systems seem to make a difference, and they certainly are thought by politicians to be worth fighting over. Indeed, the ultimate source of the failure of Hare's system to win

[70] Rae, pp. 102-3; Lakeman, pp. 165-67; and Lawrence Dodd, *Coalitions in Parliamentary Government*, Princeton, 1976, ch. 10.
[71] *Personal Representation*, pp. 8, 12. Hare even more emphatically disliked the two-party system (pp. 10-11).
[72] Stephen, *Utilitarians*, vol. III, pp. 279-80. For a similar modern view, see Rokkan, pp. 166-67.
[73] *CRG*, ch. 1, pp. 2-4.

acceptance is probably not any of the objections we have considered here (none of which seems conclusive), but the opposition of parties and groups that feel their political power threatened by a new electoral system. During the debates in Britain over various schemes of proportional representation, many of the arguments raised here were mentioned, but the overriding consideration appears to have been that both major parties believed they would lose seats and perhaps votes under any system like Hare's.[74] The "people," as Mill believed, may not be prejudiced against such a system, but the established parties, as Mill neglected to observe, not surprisingly are.[75]

ROLE OF THE REPRESENTATIVE

Mill in his earlier writings inveighed against the delegate conception of representation, according to which a representative, chosen for his views on important issues, is bound to carry out his constituents' wishes. There Mill firmly endorsed a trustee conception, which holds that a representative, chosen for his greater political knowledge and superior character, should be free to act independently of his constituents' wishes. Invoking a Platonic analogy, Mill argued that constituents should not require a representative "to act according to *their* judgment, any more than they require a physician to prescribe for them according to their own notions of medicine." The people may be qualified to judge the merits of different physicians, "whether for the body politic or natural,"

---

[74] See Butler, pp. 38-48, 58-72. For the debate in other European countries, see Rokkan, pp. 157-58, 159-61.

[75] *CRG*, ch. VII, pp. 153-54.

but they are not competent judges of different modes of treatment.[76]

But Mill's earlier writings are not, as many commentators too readily assume, a reliable guide to his mature views in *Representative Government*.[77] That the Platonic analogy does not appear here (though other passages from the earlier writings do) signals a subtle but significant shift in Mill's thinking. Even though he still rejects the pure delegate conception, he now takes a more balanced view of both conceptions. As his theory of government requires, he gives the principle of participation, as well as the principle of competence, an important place in the delineation of the role of the representative.

The principle of competence certainly implies that representatives should have considerable discretion because they are supposed to know more than their constituents. Generally, voters should seek a representative who, by past performance in politics or by reputation among recognized authorities, can be trusted to act on his or her own judgment. (If Hare's system and plural voting are not part of the constitution, it is even more important that such a representative should have great discretion.) When a representative deviates from campaign promises, he or she is not obligated to resign.[78] So that representatives will have more time to prove themselves correct in any dispute with their constituents and will be judged on their whole record, Mill does not ad-

[76] "Rationale," pp. 348-49, 364-66; and "Tocqueville" (1835), pp. 110-12. The Platonic analogy is part of the basis for Duncan's description of Mill's theory as "democratic Platonism" (*Marx and Mill*, p. 259).

[77] E.g., Duncan, *Marx and Mill*, pp. 261-62.

[78] *CRG*, ch. XII, pp. 232-34, 237.

vocate annual or frequent elections, as his father and Bentham did.[79]

However, it is "no less important" that the representative be responsible to his constituents, as the protective argument for participation stresses. Interpreters of Mill fail to notice that the principle of participation constrains the application of the principle of competence here in a number of ways. First, constituents may require pledges of the representative if, because of adverse social circumstances or faulty institutions such as existed at least in Mill's time, they are forced to accept a representative who is "under the influence of partialities hostile to their interest." Mill asks:

> Can we blame an elector of the poorer classes, who has only the choice among two or three rich men, for requiring from the one he votes for, a pledge to those measures which he considers as a test of emancipation from the class-interests of the rich?[80]

Second, when a relatively unknown person is elected for the first time, voters may make "conformity to [their] own sentiments the primary requisite." Third, *all* representatives must state in advance the opinions on which they intend to act, and must fully explain any subsequent deviations from them. Without such statements and explanations, voters cannot *rationally* defer to their representatives. A representative should also ensure that the opinions of his or her constituents are effectively expressed in Parliament whether the repre-

[79] *CRG*, ch. XI, 220-21. Cf. Bentham, *Radical Reform Bill*, in *Works*, vol. III, pp. 561-62; and James Mill, *Essay on Government*, ch. VII, pp. 69-72.

[80] *CRG*, ch. XII, pp. 236-37, 230. This constraint on the trustee conception also appeared in the early writings ("Rationale," p. 366).

sentative agrees with them or not. Otherwise, Parliament would not be a place where "every interest and shade of opinion in the country" can have its cause pleaded.[81] Third, the most important constraint is that representatives should not act in opposition to their constituents' "fundamental convictions" (or "primary notions of right"). Constituents would be justified in dismissing a representative who disagreed with them, for example, on policy toward foreign aggression (when an assured majority for their view does not exist in Parliament).[82] The educative argument for participation may also limit the representative's discretion. Mill rejects indirect or two-stage elections because they require voters merely to give their "general power of attorney" to a representative to act for them and do not encourage voters to take into account "political considerations" ("opinions and measures, or political men"). This limited kind of participation would fail to develop the "public spirit and political intelligence" of citizens.[83] For the same reason, we could say that constituents' political opinions ought to play a significant part in their choice of a representative and should influence the representative's subsequent behavior (though Mill does not explicitly use this argument in connection with direct elections).

Had Mill given free rein to the principle of competence, his conception of the role of the representative would have looked much like Burke's, except that the aristocracy, in Mill's opinion, had forfeited the claim to

[81] *CRG*, ch. XII, pp. 234-35; ch. v, pp. 104-5.

[82] *CRG*, ch. XII, pp. 235-36. Mill's conception of the representative's role thus is not based, as Pitkin suggests it is (p. 205), on the distinction between constituents' short-range and long-range interests.

[83] *CRG*, ch. IX, p. 190.

115

competence that Burke granted it. Although Burke expected representatives to consider their constituents' "feelings" and to look after local interests in certain cases, he generally gave representatives complete freedom to act as they saw fit in pursuit of the general interest.[84] Indeed, Mill, as an M.P. from Westminster for three years, behaved himself much like a Burkean representative (though the "advanced" causes to which he devoted himself were hardly ones Burke would have approved). Mill nevertheless could not have thought that all, or even most, representatives should act exactly as he did, failing to speak on most of the leading controversial issues of his day.[85] For in his theory of government, as we have noticed, Mill is committed by the principle of participation to give constituents a great deal more to say about how their representatives should act than Burke or Mill himself as an M.P. was prepared to permit. Moreover, Mill must have been aware that many of the so-called independent M.P.s were actually spokesmen for groups promoting various special interests.[86]

The exact balance between the two elements in Mill's conception of representation must be worked out in practice, according to the particular issues at stake and the social and political conditions that his theory

[84] Edmund Burke, "Speech to the Electors of Bristol" and "Appeal from the New to the Old Whigs," in *Burke's Politics*, ed. Ross Hoffman and Paul Levack, New York, 1959, esp. pp. 115-16, 397-98. Generally, on Burke's idea of representation, see Ernest Barker, *Essays on Government*, 2d ed., Oxford, 1951; and Pitkin, pp. 168-89, 206-7.

[85] On Mill's parliamentary career, see Packe, pp. 446-57, 473-74. However, Mill considered his behavior to be a general model in certain respects—e.g., his refusal to pay his own election expenses or to allow them to exceed certain limits (*CRG*, ch. x, pp. 213-17; and *Thoughts on Parliamentary Reform*, pp. 16-19).

[86] See Samuel H. Beer, *British Politics in the Collectivist Age*, New York, 1969, pp. 61-65.

specifies. We cannot, he believes, stipulate theoretically a positive duty defining the relation between constituents and their representatives.[87] In this respect, Hanna Pitkin, who presents the best modern analysis of the mandate-independence controversy, ends up very close to Mill. She maintains that there is "no rational basis" for choosing between the delegate and trustee conceptions *tout court*. The concept of representation implies that normally the representative's judgment and his constituents' wishes coincide, and when they do not, we need more information about the particular case to decide the question. Pitkin suggests that this is why public opinion polls get equivocal results when they ask, "Ought a representative to do what he thinks best or what his constituents want?"[88] When representatives themselves are asked how they conceive of their roles, the more sophisticated of them refuse to see a "simple choice between independent judgment on the one hand and constituency wishes on the other."[89] The behavior of Congressmen, furthermore, varies depending on the issues. The roll-call votes of Congressmen correspond to their constituents' opinions more closely on civil rights (which, in Mill's terms, might be seen as a matter of "fundamental convictions") than they do on social welfare issues and foreign policy.[90]

[87] *CRG*, ch. XII, p. 231.   [88] Pitkin, pp. 165-66.

[89] Charles O. Jones, "Representation in Congress," *American Political Science Review* 55 (Dec. 1961), p. 365. A study of city councilors in the San Francisco area found that a majority think of themselves as "trustees," but that the "trustees" are more likely to respond to special-interest groups than "non-trustee" representatives (Heinz Eulau and Kenneth Prewitt, *Labyrinths of Democracy*, Indianapolis, 1973, pp. 407-23).

[90] Warren E. Miller and Donald E. Stokes, "Constituency Influence in Congress," *American Political Science Review* 57 (March 1963), pp. 45-56.

In the very different constitutional context of Britain, M.P.s do not think of themselves as either trustees or delegates in quite the traditional sense. Their ideas of democracy generally deprecate the extensive popular participation that a delegate conception presupposes (though they do look after the specific problems that individual constituents may have with the government). And their commitment to party government usually precludes the possibility of acting independently as trustees themselves.[91] The party leaders in effect become the trustees, but they presumably do not see this role as normally in conflict with their constituents' wishes. Nor does such a conception rule out representation by interest groups acting through parties or directly on the government—now a common process in Britain as well as in other democracies.[92] Mill gave little attention to this process, although (as we saw earlier) he recognized, and approved, the growing influence of political organizations of many kinds (the "power of combination"). His theory could accommodate the representation of group interests as another kind of apparent interest; they would be filtered through the institutions of representative government just as the interests of individuals are.

Another feature of some modern democracies—party discipline—cannot be so easily appended to Mill's account of representation. In many democracies and especially in Britain, party discipline largely overshadows any choice between a representative's independence and

[91] Cf. Robert D. Putnam, *The Beliefs of Politicians*, New Haven, 1973, pp. 182-90, 235; Anthony Barker and Michael Rush, *The Member of Parliament and His Information*, London, 1970, pp. 168-204; and Beer, pp. 69-70.

[92] Beer, pp. 71-79, 318-51.

his constituents' wishes. Mill did not seriously discuss party discipline probably because party voting in Commons was infrequent until about the time *Representative Government* was published and did not approach modern levels until the 1890s.[93] But what Mill's attitude toward this development would have been can be easily inferred from his general opinion of party government. Mill dislikes strong party government for three reasons. First, it is wrong that

> all the opinions, feelings and interests of all members of the community should be merged in the single consideration of which party shall predominate. We require a House of Commons which shall be a fitting representative of all the feelings of the people, and not merely their party feelings.[94]

Moreover, highly disciplined parties would weaken the tie that Mill thought so important to maintain between voters and their representatives; in modern Britain that tie is indeed weak, since most voters have little awareness of anything more than their M.P.'s party affiliation.[95] Second, the process by which parties select candidates allows neither for extensive participation nor for the choice of the most competent individuals. Mill's observation that only a small group of party leaders choose candidates still holds today, and his related complaint,

[93] A. Lawrence Lowell, *The Government of England*, New York, 1908, vol. II, p. 78; Beer, pp. 184-85, 257, 262-63; and Hugh Berrington, "Partisanship and Dissidence in the Nineteenth-Century House of Commons," *Parliamentary Affairs* 21 (Autumn 1968), pp. 338-74.

[94] *Personal Representation*, p. 12. On Mill's earlier disillusionment with party activity, see Hamburger, pp. 242-72.

[95] Butler and Stokes, pp. 355-56.

that these party leaders tend to pick candidates who are uncontroversial and distinguished mostly for their party loyalty, continues to be repeated.[96] The third and most important reason Mill could not approve of strong party government is that it undermines the ability of a competent minority in Parliament to sway the opinions and votes of the rest of the assembly, independently of the government. With highly disciplined parties, no amount of discussion and agitation would change many minds in the deliberations, and the independent representative would not have much impact.[97]

The conventional view now approves of strong parties in Britain and sees them as essential for effective, stable government, or as important for implementing the broad interests of the working classes.[98] Yet, as A. H. Birch has pointed out, this view still lacks an adequate theoretical justification.[99] Especially as long as we lack a satisfactory theory of current practice, we can still learn a great deal from Mill's theory, standing as it does on some points in critical opposition to modern practice. Even the advocates of strong party government admit some of the dangers of which Mill warned, and his warnings are also echoed in criticisms of proposals that would inject some British party discipline into the

[96] *CRG*, ch. VII, pp. 136-37; *Personal Representation*, p. 8. See Austin Ranney, *Pathways to Parliament*, Madison, Wis., 1965, esp. pp. 273-74; and Michael Rush, *The Selection of Parliamentary Candidates*, London, 1969, pp. 276, 279, 281. Another practice that Mill criticized—that of giving preference to candidates who would pay their own election expenses—was not prohibited by law until 1948.

[97] Cf. *CRG*, ch. VI, p. 129.

[98] Robert T. McKenzie, *British Political Parties*, 2d ed., New York, 1964, esp. pp. 645-46; and Beer, pp. 86-88, 98-102, 349-51.

[99] A. H. Birch, *Responsible and Representative Government*, London, 1964, p. 121 (reaffirmed in his *Representation*, p. 100).

American system.[100] At the least, then, Mill's theory points to some weaknesses in the modern practice of representation and provides some standards by which it may be assessed.

ROLE OF THE REPRESENTATIVE ASSEMBLY

The representative assembly should control the business of government, not actually do it, Mill asserts. Not only should the assembly not intervene in administrative matters and personnel appointments, as most people admit, but it also should not attempt to formulate and amend legislation. A representative assembly cannot take into account all of the many factors that should go into the framing of a law, and its "clumsy hands" produce confusion and contradiction when the body tries to amend legislation.[101] Mill would assign the principal job of framing laws to a Legislative Commission, whose members would be appointed by the Crown for (renewable) five-year terms, subject to removal by Parliament.[102] The Commission would prepare legislation at the specific request of the representative assembly; but the assembly could only pass, reject, or return a bill to

[100] McKenzie, p. 643; and Austin Ranney and Willmoore Kendall, *Democracy and the American Party System*, New York, 1956, pp. 527-33.

[101] *CRG*, ch. v, pp. 89-100. Earlier comments on this general problem include "Tocqueville," in *DD*, pp. 159-61; and "Vindication of the French Revolution of February, 1848," in *DD*, vol. III, pp. 76-80. His final opinion appears in the *Autobiography*, ch. VII, pp. 185-86.

[102] Mill suggests that a transformed House of Lords might serve as the Commission, but this would appear to create a conflict of interest, since he assigns to *both* Houses the powers of dismissing and instructing the Commission (*CRG*, ch. v, pp. 318-19).

the Commission for reconsideration.[103] That these limited powers would constitute the sole legislative role of the assembly would in no way detract from the democratic character of the constitution, for even Athenian democracy accepted similar limitations.[104] The assembly would of course retain the power to expel the government from office, but even this power could not usually be exercised without bringing about the dissolution of the assembly. Mill would even favor the American practice of making the election of the chief executive independent of the assembly, were it not that the quality of persons chosen would be lower and the time spent on electioneering much greater. A chief executive elected by a parliament for a fixed term would, in Mill's opinion, be one way of achieving the advantages of the American system without its disadvantages.[105]

Reflecting on Mill's division of legislative functions, one is tempted to associate the Commission with the principle of competence and the assembly with the principle of participation. The point of the Commission, after all, is to supply instrumental competence, and the assembly, by "controlling" the business of government, carries out part of the protective aim of participation. The Commission embodies "the element of intelligence . . . Parliament represents that of will."[106] But the struc-

[103] *CRG*, ch. v, pp. 100-101. A nascent version of the proposal is in Bentham's *Constitutional Code*, p. 191; but one closer to Mill's is suggested by Edwin Chadwick, who eagerly reports Mill's approval of it (see B. W. Richardson [ed.], *The Health of Nations*, London, 1887, vol. I, pp. 133-40). There is no evidence that Mill derived the idea from Chadwick, however.

[104] *CRG*, ch. v, pp. 101-2. See Ernest Barker's notes in *The Politics of Aristotle*, Oxford, 1962, pp. 128, 149, 168.

[105] *CRG*, ch. v, p. 105; ch. xiv, pp. 258-61.

[106] *CRG*, ch. v, p. 101.

ture of Mill's theory is more complicated than this schema suggests because here, as elsewhere, each institution is supposed to realize aspects of both participation and competence. Administration and the formulation of laws are separated from the assembly not only to recognize competence but also to establish individual responsibility for administrative and legislative action, as the protective argument for participation requires. Administrators and Commissioners are more likely to feel personal responsibility (and to be held accountable) for the detailed, technical business of government than would representatives if they were to conduct this business.[107] Similarly, competence is not the monopoly of the administrators and Commissioners. At the least, some representatives are expected to manifest moral competence in their deliberations and decisions.

The notion that the government has the responsibility to present a legislative program was only beginning to be accepted in Mill's time; individual M.P.s still initiated a great deal of legislation. Although expert advisory commissions helped draft some bills, Parliament often altered them even in detail.[108] Now, however, Mill's definition of the limited role of the assembly much more closely fits virtually all parliamentary systems, as executives have assumed more and more power in the legislative process.[109] Many observers defend this development for precisely the reasons that Mill gave.[110]

[107] *CRG*, ch. v, pp. 95, 106-7; cf. ch. xiv, pp. 251-52.

[108] S. A. Walkland, *The Legislative Process in Great Britain*, London, 1968, pp. 12-16, 55-56; and John P. Mackintosh, *The British Cabinet*, London, 1962, pp. 250-52.

[109] Wheare, pp. 167, 219-27; Walkland, pp. 68-69; and Adams, pp. 82-83, 159-60; and Inter-Parliamentary Union, *Parliaments*, London, 1966, pp. 149-51.

[110] Walkland, p. 103; and Adams, pp. 198-99.

But others worry that it has gone too far. They criticize, for example, the growth of delegated legislation enacted by the executive with little parliamentary scrutiny, and, without intending to reverse these trends, they propose reforms such as the creation of specialized committees, like those established in Britain in 1966.[111] The critics, too, could find support in Mill's theory since most of their proposals are meant merely to strengthen parliamentary control over legislation, not to return to Parliament the task of formulating legislation. Moreover, some of the specific criticisms of the executive's legislative performance—its remoteness and its excessive devotion to precedent—are the same criticisms that Mill made of the bureaucracy.[112]

The second important role of the representative assembly, according to Mill, is to be "the nation's Committee of Grievances, and its Congress of Opinions." The assembly is "to indicate wants, to be an organ for popular demands, and a place of adverse discussion for all opinions relating to public matters . . . [and] to check by criticism, and eventually by withdrawing their support, those high public officers who really conduct the public business. . . ."[113] A properly constituted assembly ensures that all interests and opinions will be expressed and thus enjoy a reasonable chance of being protected, as the principle of participation demands. The deliberations should also have an educative effect not only on the representatives but also on their constituents, who, though they are usually only spectators to the delibera-

[111] Political and Economic Planning, *Reforming the Commons*, London, 1965, vol. 31; John P. Mackintosh, "Reform of the Commons: The Case for Specialized Committees," in Gerhard Loewenberg (ed.), *Modern Parliaments*, Chicago, 1971, pp. 33-61; and Walkland, pp. 18, 44-45, 52-53.

[112] Walkland, p. 18.

[113] *CRG*, ch. v, pp. 104-6. Cf. Walkland, pp. 68-69.

tions, can identify with their representatives. Those who lose out in the parliamentary debates will be able to see that their interests were "set aside not by a mere act of will, but for what are thought superior reasons."[114]

Since the deliberations end in votes on legislation, it matters a great deal that the more competent representatives, who are more likely to pursue the general interest, carry considerable weight. But how, in a body teeming with conflicting opinions, can the competent few hope to prevail?

> The reason why, in any tolerably constituted society, justice and the general interest mostly in the end carry their point, is that the separate and selfish interests of mankind are almost always divided; . . . and those who are governed by higher considerations, though too few and weak to prevail against the whole of the others, usually after sufficient discussion and agitation become strong enough to turn the balance in favour of the body of private interests which is on the same side with them.[115]

This solution to the problem has been criticized as an "act of faith" because it allegedly rests on two implausible assumptions—that the selfish interests balance, and that a minority acts in the general interest.[116] But for Mill it is not a matter of faith, but rather of very stringent conditions that he imposes on the political process. Mill's solution will work only if "the representative system could be made ideally perfect" and if the society is not divided by "strong antipathies of race, language, or nationality." If society is not so divided, the assump-

114 CRG, ch. v, p. 104. Cf. Rousseau, Contrat social, Bk. IV, ch. 2.
115 CRG, ch. VI, p. 129.   116 Pitkin, p. 203.

tion that selfish interests will coalesce into two classes —laborers, on the one hand, and employers and professionals, on the other—is not so implausible.[117] Indeed, as many social scientists have confirmed, such class divisions are a chief basis of modern British politics, and although the classes may not always balance in Parliament or the electorate at any given time, they may tend to do so over time.[118] That the independent minority have little scope to influence the proceedings in modern parliaments is, as we have seen, largely a consequence of party government, in which Mill put no great faith. To sustain competence in the representative assembly, a whole set of conditions is necessary: for example, a system of Personal Representation, rational deference on the part of voters, and the progressive improvement of the political intelligence of citizens and representatives as a democracy matures. Because modern democracies generally do not meet Mill's conditions, his solution cannot be expected to work in them at present. But this consequence may say more about the shortcomings of modern democracies than it does about any deficiencies in Mill's theory of government. Mill's hope that his stringent conditions would be fulfilled may have been excessive. But that this optimism is unwarranted hardly refutes his contention that if the conditions were met, the legislative process would be more likely to function as his theory prescribes.

LOCAL GOVERNMENT

The principles of participation and competence both come into play in the institutions of local government,

[117] *CRG*, ch. VI, p. 128.

[118] Pulzer, p. 102; Butler and Stokes, pp. 77-78, 173; and Robert Alford, *Party and Society*, Chicago, 1963, pp. 101-21. But cf. Richard Rose, "Class and Party Divisions," pp. 129-62.

but here the former carry greater weight than the latter because the opportunities for more active participation are greater, and the need for a high degree of competence is less urgent than in national government. Local government furnishes citizens a chance to serve, by selection or rotation, in numerous executive offices, where political "thinking cannot be all done by proxy." The local executive officers cannot be controlled by an assembly of the entire local citizenry, as in New England; that system works only under special conditions, such as a high level of prosperity, which give everyone a strong interest in local government. Generally, executives should be controlled, Mill insists, by local representative assemblies, which provide financial support, appoint the chief executive, and hold him responsible for the performance of other local authorities. Mill would therefore object, as some recent critics have, to the now common practice of local council committees' directly holding chief officers of departments accountable.[119] The same procedures for electing representatives apply to this assembly as to the national assembly, and the "same reasons operate . . . but with still greater force, for giving them a widely democratic basis. . . ." However, only persons who pay property taxes may vote—a stipulation that appears to make some citizens who are eligible to vote in national elections ineligible to do so in local elections.[120]

The principle of competence manifests itself in local government in two ways that differ somewhat from those in national government. Once again, Mill turns to plural voting and this time even allows "a mere money

[119] *CRG*, ch. xv, pp. 274-77, 285; "Tocqueville" (1835), pp. 100-101; and J. K. Friend and W. N. Jessop, *Local Government and Strategic Choice*, London, 1969, pp. 47-48, 243-49.

[120] *CRG*, ch. xv, pp. 277-78. This restriction on local suffrage was not lifted until after World War II.

qualification" to justify extra votes because the "honest and frugal dispensation of money forms so much larger a part of the business of the local, than of the national body. . . ." Also, by permitting justices of the peace to serve *ex officio* in smaller local bodies like the Board of Guardians, Mill believes that a better educated class can check the class interests of the farmers and smaller shopkeepers. Such special representation is not necessary in the larger county councils because the importance of the business alone is a great enough incentive to attract the services of competent individuals.[121] Modern students of local government have called for the abolition of the vestiges of this special representation (for example, aldermen who are appointed to local councils by elected councilmen) because these appointees tend to acquire excessive power and resist desirable change.[122]

How should authority be divided between local and national government? The answer, Mill thinks, is obvious enough in the case of "purely local business" (such as paving, lighting, water supply, drainage and market regulations), in which the rest of the country has only an indirect interest and which does not need uniform regulation. Other matters (such as law enforcement) are "so universal a concern, and so much a matter of general science" that they ought to be administered by national authorities. As Mill recognizes, these criteria do not cover many of the important problems of government, such as those that are of national concern but must be directly managed by local authorities. Indeed, some of Mill's own examples of local business might

[121] *CRG*, ch. xv, p. 278.
[122] L. J. Sharpe, *Why Local Democracy*, Fabian Tract 361, London, 1965, pp. 32-33.

today fall in this category. Hence, the question becomes not *which* activities belong to each level of government, but how much authority each level should have in the conduct of *every* activity.[123] This question, it should be noted, is distinct from the general question of the proper limits of governmental action, which does not turn on whether the action is taken by local or central authorities. In *Representative Government* Mill does not discuss this general problem because it is "in no way peculiar to representative government."[124]

A rough guide to the division of authority between local and central government is that the "principal business of the central authority should be to give instruction, of the local authority to apply it. Power may be localised, but knowledge . . . must be centralised."[125] The Poor Law of 1834, which Mill continued to defend against its critics (who included some of the Philosophic Radicals), is his favorite example of the proper balance between centralization and decentralization. The central board sets the general policies for poor relief and makes sure that any violations are turned over to the courts, the local boards, or the local representative bodies. The local authorities retain a great deal of discretion, and Mill strenuously insists that poor relief is primarily a local matter. His interpretation of the operation of the Poor Law appears to be correct, though the legislation triggered a process that, as conceptions of

[123] *CRG*, ch. xv, pp. 286-88. An approach very similar to Mill's is John P. Mackintosh's in *Devolution of Power*, Harmondsworth, 1968, pp. 45-52.

[124] *CRG*, ch. xv, p. 274. Mill cites *Liberty*, ch. v; and *Political Economy*, Bk. v, ch. xi.

[125] *CRG*, ch. xv, p. 291. Cf. *Liberty*, ch. v, pp. 204-5; and *Political Economy*, Bk. v, ch. xi, § 4, pp. 940-41.

the government's responsibility for welfare broadened, eventually placed a great deal of authority for social welfare in the hands of the central departments.[126]

Mill advocates a balance between centralization and decentralization in order to serve the aims of both participation and competence. The central government has access to more information and better minds and thus is in a better position to realize greater competence. Local citizens have a more direct interest in the results of many decisions and are better able to discover and punish any abuses by local authorities. As we saw in Chapter 1, some evidence supports Mill's claim that the activity of citizens in local politics better fulfills the protective and educative goals of participation. But the central government has no monopoly on competence, and local government has none on participation. The central government is deficient in "detailed knowledge of local persons and things," in which local citizens may have superior competence. Local government, more often the "slave of vulgar prejudices," may oppress local minorities whose interests would be better protected by the more impartial authority of the central government.[127] Mill's belief that minority interests may be better protected in larger units is supported by a recent study indicating that as the size of a political unit increases, the "likelihood of persistent and overt opposition to majority views also increases."[128] The central

---

[126] "Centralisation," pp. 351-52; *Liberty*, ch. v, pp. 205-7; and "Tocqueville," in *DD*, p. 104. See Sidney and Beatrice Webb, *English Poor Law History*, London, 1929, vol. I, pp. 100-101, 189-90. Cf. Samuel Mencher, *Poor Law to Poverty Program*, Pittsburgh, 1967, pp. 93-129.

[127] *CRG*, ch. xv, pp. 289-91; and "Centralisation," p. 351.

[128] Dahl and Tufte, pp. 89-108.

government therefore has a role, even concerning matters of detail, in protecting interests in accordance with the principle of participation. Finally, the educative function of participation needs support from the generally more competent central authorities because, Mill insists, civic education, especially on the local level, requires competent "teachers," who are in shorter supply in local government. Mill's complaint about the low caliber of leaders in local politics is still often repeated today.[129]

Thus, because the values of competence and participation both can be realized to some extent in both local and national government, the division between the levels of government should not be rigid. The balance between centralization and decentralization has to be worked out in practice, varying according to the policies in question and the historical circumstances. If Mill's conclusion seems equivocal, it is so because the nature of the problem admits of no simple generalizations. The most thorough recent study of the relation between local and central authorities in Britain comes to a conclusion remarkably similar to Mill's.[130]

While Mill seeks to strike a balance, he stresses (in his mature writings) decentralization more than Bentham and some of the Philosophic Radicals did, and he is very surprised when he is branded an "apostle of centralisation," a characterization that some commentators

[129] *CRG*, ch. xv, pp. 281-83, 293-94. See Sharpe, *Why Local Democracy*, pp. 1-2, 31-33; "Elected Representatives in Local Government," *British Journal of Sociology* 13 (Sept. 1962), pp. 201-8; and Samuel Humes and Eileen Martin, *The Structure of Local Government Throughout the World*, The Hague, 1961, p. 165.

[130] J.A.G. Griffith, *Central Departments and Local Authorities*, Toronto, 1966, pp. 507-8. Cf. Humes and Martin, pp. 507-8.

continue mistakenly to apply to him.[131] It was the influence of Tocqueville, especially his emphasis on the educative potential of smaller political units, that kept Mill from overvaluing centralization.[132] For some of the same reasons, Mill takes a favorable view of federalism, at least of the American variety, which gives the central government direct authority over individual citizens. Unlike Bentham, Mill does not assert a general superiority of "government simple."[133] On the contrary, he holds that "portions of mankind who are not fitted, or not disposed, to live under the same internal government" should under certain conditions choose federal government. Mill even praises Calhoun's *Disquisition on Government* and, without himself endorsing the proposition that each state should have a veto on acts of the federal government, implies that it is acceptable where the feelings of a community support it.[134]

Mill foresaw that new social and economic conditions, technological developments, and the increasing scale of activities in modern society would generate new needs for central legislation and regulation by the state. But he thought that this trend toward centralization could be prevented from destroying local initiative if central

[131] Cf. Bentham, *Constitutional Code*, pp. 640-43. Mill is regarded as a centralizer by René Millet, "Le Parti Radical en Angleterre: un manifeste de M. Stuart Mill," *Revue des Deux Mondes* 97 (Feb. 15, 1872), pp. 932-59. Mill's brief comment on this article is in his letter to John Elliot Cairnes (April 22, 1872) in *Later Letters, CW*, vol. XVII, pp. 1887-88. A recent commentator who identifies Mill with Benthamite views on centralization is William Wickwar, *The Political Theory of Local Government*, Columbia, S.C., 1970, p. 21.

[132] *Autobiography*, ch. VI, pp. 115-16; and "Tocqueville," in *DD*, p. 104.

[133] Bentham, *Constitutional Code*, pp. 644-47.

[134] *CRG*, ch. XVII, pp. 306, 311, 315.

authorities would confine themselves to general over-sight, rather than direct control.[135] The *formal* relation between central and local authorities in Britain has changed little since the Acts of 1888 and 1894, upon which the influence of Mill's thought is said to have been strong.[136] But stricter controls by the central government accompany the grants that are now the most important single source of revenue for local government.[137] Other trends, such as the rise of nationalized industries, reinforce central authority. Centralization in nearly all modern democracies has outpaced Mill's expectations, and the "decline of local self-government" has become a familiar refrain of social scientists and social critics. Echoing Mill, some British reformers urge that local government be strengthened and that effective participation in local government be stimulated.[138] And in the United States, for both Mill and Tocqueville a model of effective local government in the nineteenth century, theorists and reformers now call for greater community control in the cities, marshalling arguments much like Mill's.[139]

However, if the objective is to strengthen participa-

[135] "Centralisation," pp. 345-47.

[136] Josef Redlich and Francis W. Hirst, *The History of Local Government in England*, London, 1970, p. 189.

[137] Cf. Alan T. Peacock and Jack Wiseman, *The Growth of Public Expenditure in the United Kingdom*, Princeton, 1961, pp. 96-120; and Central Statistical Office, *Annual Abstract of Statistics, 1975*, London, 1975, p. 371. Generally, see Griffith, pp. 534-36.

[138] Dilys M. Hill, *Participating in Local Affairs*, Harmondsworth, 1970; and Ioan B. Rees, *Government by Community*, London, 1971, pp. 75-136, 110-11.

[139] E.g., George Frederickson (ed.), *Neighborhood Control in the 1970's*, New York, 1973; and Douglas T. Yates, *Neighborhood Democracy*, Lexington, Mass., 1973.

tion, the present relatively small local governments are not necessarily the best, or the only, units on which to concentrate. As Mill points out, smaller local units are more easily dominated by narrow oligarchies and are less able to deal with many problems that affect them because the problems extend beyond their jurisdictions. Mill therefore maintains that "different kinds of local business may require different areas of representation," thus anticipating a conclusion of the major recent study of relationships between the scale of societies and democratic politics.[140] Strains of Mill's arguments also appear in the proposals of a long line of writers who would enlarge local governments or establish regional units of government to deal more competently and responsibly with modern problems.[141] And much of the rationale for the Redcliffe-Maud Report, which would drastically reduce the number of local authorities, can be found in Mill's theory.[142]

Mill's theory of government, mixing both the principle of participation and the principle of competence in each institution of a democracy, does not stipulate a determinate balance for the values expressed by these principles. However, it does suggest which characteristics the institutions should have to realize these values, and it indicates ways in which both kinds of values may be combined in the same institution. The institutions give the competent minority opportunities for greater influence than they would have in a democracy with a

[140] *CRG*, ch. xv, pp. 281-84; and Dahl and Tufte, p. 135.

[141] G.D.H. Cole, *The Future of Local Government*, London, 1921, esp. pp. 155-56; W. A. Robson, *Local Government in Crisis*, London, 1966, pp. 69-73, 93, 146-48; Mackintosh, *Devolution*, pp. 45-52; and Humes and Martin, pp. 162-64.

[142] Royal Commission on Local Government in England, *Report*, vol. i, Cmnd. 4040, London, 1969.

simple majoritarian electoral system, a delegate conception of representation, an assembly that writes legislation, and a highly decentralized government. But the institutions are also designed to ensure, through various kinds of citizen participation, that the competent minority acquire significant influence only with the rational concurrence of most citizens and that political activity remain extensive. Although Mill leaves a great deal to practical judgment and action in shaping the final mixture of the principles of participation and competence in particular circumstances, the basic structure of his theory is remarkably comprehensive and systematic. The properties he ascribes to each institution or process of representative democracy flow from the principles of participation and competence that form the core of his theory of government.

4

The Theory of Development

"[A]ny general theory or philosophy of politics," Mill writes, "supposes a previous theory of human progress . . . [which] is the same thing with a philosophy of history."[1] Although Mill never elaborates a theory of this kind in *Representative Government,* he implicitly relies on one at many crucial points in his argument, and he sometimes explicitly appeals to one as well. This chapter explains Mill's view of the nature of such a theory and its significance for his democratic theory.

Neither "progress" nor "history," however, is a suitable designation for the theory as Mill uses it in *Representative Government.* There is nothing wrong with the idea of progress, Mill thinks, even as the whole basis for a criterion of good government. The trouble is with the word "progress," which suggests "moving onward, whereas the meaning of it here is quite as much the prevention of falling back."[2] When Mill allows himself to use the word in the *Logic,* he assigns it an unorthodox meaning, one that is not necessarily supposed to connote improvement.[3] It would be less misleading to call Mill's theory a philosophy of history, as he sometimes does himself, were it not that "history" fails to capture Mill's emphasis on the future course of human development.

[1] *Autobiography,* ch. v, p. 97.
[2] *CRG,* ch. ii, p. 26.
[3] *Logic,* Bk. vi, ch. x, § 3, p. 914.

More appropriate is the term "development," which is somewhat more neutral than "progress" and more general than "history."[4]

USES OF A THEORY OF DEVELOPMENT

Mill does not believe that anyone—not even Comte, who came closest—has successfully created a full-blown theory of development that would explain the broad course of social and political change. Nevertheless, he thinks we can discern, from the rudiments of a theory of development, some of the general features of the process of development to which we can appeal in defending a conception of representative government. There are at least three ways in which a theory of development assists Mill's theory of democracy.

Since Mill wishes to urge that representative government be adopted (under appropriate conditions) and that it be improved, he needs a theory of development to justify the possibility of establishing political institutions and changing them over time. The opening pages of *Representative Government* contrast two views of political development that deal with these possibilities.[5] A mechanist view regards the development of political institutions as "wholly an affair of invention and contrivance." Men need only determine the ends of government and the means by which they may be most effec-

---

[4] Mill occasionally uses "development" in this way (e.g., *Logic*, p. 915). Comte, from whom comes Mill's distinction between the two senses of progress (cumulative change and improvement), recommends the term "développement," which he believes designates an incontestable fact without conveying any "appréciation morale" (*Cours de philosophie positive*, Paris, 1877, vol. IV, p. 264).

[5] *CRG*, ch. I, pp. 1-4.

tively attained, and then persuade others to implement the means. This essentially was James Mill's view, though the younger Mill does not say so here.[6] The "naturalistic theory," in contrast, considers the development of institutions as "a sort of spontaneous product" and holds that government "cannot be constructed by premeditated design." On this view, a theory of development could only acquaint us with the "natural properties" of institutions and help us "adapt ourselves to them." Both views, taken by themselves, are absurd, Mill thinks. We do not choose a contrivance solely because it is the best per se; we consider, for example, whether those who will use it have the knowledge required to use it properly. Macaulay's criticism of Mill's father hovers over the discussion again, now restraining Mill from fully embracing the mechanist view.[7] But neither can we really believe that "mankind have absolutely no range of choice as to the government they will live under." Characteristically, Mill extracts the partial truth from each of the two views; but this time the result is not an even-handed balance, for he ends up closer to the mechanist view.[8] The truth in the naturalistic theory, stripped of its sentimentality, turns out to be merely that a government must satisfy three fundamental conditions.[9] These are equivalent to Mill's general condi-

[6] Cf. *Autobiography*, ch. v, pp. 94-95.

[7] Macaulay, "Mill," pp. 284-85, 321-22.

[8] Cf. *CRG*, ch. xviii, pp. 347-49. To this extent Michael Oakeshott's mechanist interpretation of Mill has some foundation; however, Mill does not hold, as Oakeshott suggests he does, a view "in which institutions and procedures appear as pieces of machinery designed to achieve a purpose settled in advance, instead of as manners of behavior which are meaningless when separated from their context . . ." (*Rationalism in Politics*, London, 1962, pp. 130-31).

[9] *CRG*, ch. i, p. 9.

tions for the stability of any government. Within the limits of these rather minimal conditions, individuals can, by the efficacy of human will, introduce a form of government into society and make rational improvements in it over time.[10] A theory of development that recognizes the possibility of change by human design thus supports a democratic theory that would modify government to fulfill, for example, the principles of participation and competence.

Mill relies on a theory of development in a second way also. His criteria for a good form of government refer in part to those aspects of government that encourage improvement—the promotion of the "virtue and intelligence of the people themselves."[11] A government works toward this end by furthering participation and competence. Without a theory of development Mill could offer only a static criterion of government—one that assesses governments according to how well they perform at any particular time, but not how well their present performance promotes future improvement. It has often been noted that much writing about democracy in recent years embodies a static conception of democracy, emphasizing the conditions that support stability rather than reform or change.[12] Aware of the importance of a theory of development, Mill escapes this parochial orientation. Elsewhere Mill observes that many people tend to assume that whatever character a society (or an individual) exhibits at a particular time is the character

[10] *CRG*, ch. I, pp. 11-13.

[11] *CRG*, ch. II, p. 30.

[12] Christian Bay, "Politics and Pseudopolitics," *American Political Science Review* 59 (March 1965), p. 47; Stephen W. Rousseas and James Farganis, "American Politics and the End of Ideology," *British Journal of Sociology* 14 (Dec. 1963), pp. 347-62; and Walker, pp. 288, 292.

it naturally or inevitably tends to have. A theory of development saves us from this error by drawing our attention to the conditions that, over time, have made people the way they are and therefore can, if altered, make them different from what they are.[13] With a theory of development, furthermore, Mill can attend to the requirements for improvement and reform even while analyzing the conditions of stability.

Finally, a theory of development assists in understanding transitions from one stage to another in the process of improving representative democracy. In its most general form, such a theory would also show the intermediate stages that communities must traverse before they become fit for representative democracy. This is the subject of much of the contemporary literature on political development.[14] But it is not Mill's subject here presumably because, like the question of "what kind of government is suited to every known state of society," it would require a general treatise on political science, exceeding the more limited aim Mill has set for himself.[15] Not only here, but generally, Mill is interested in using a theory of development much more for changing the future than for explaining the past, and consequently he focuses on the development of more advanced democracies. Although Mill sometimes refers to his theory as a "historical method," he sees its chief value

[13] *Subjection of Women*, ch. I, pp. 39-42.

[14] E.g., Dahl, *Polyarchy*, esp. pp. 1-16. Other writers on development focus almost exclusively on the transition process—for example, by examining the conditions under which political development can keep pace with social and economic development (see, e.g., Samuel P. Huntington, *Political Order in Changing Societies*, New Haven, 1968, pp. 78-92).

[15] *CRG*, ch. II, pp. 40, 43-44.

in determining what artificial means may be used, and to what extent, to accelerate the natural progress in so far as it is beneficial; to compensate for whatever may be its inherent inconveniences or disadvantages; and to guard against the dangers or accidents to which our species is exposed from the necessary incidents of progression.[16]

In the service of a democratic theory, a theory of development thus can identify the direction and rate in which society is likely to move and the method and causal agency by which that natural course may be modified or reinforced. More specifically, a theory of development can discover trends that impede or promote the realization of the principles of competence and participation, as well as the reduction of the tension between them in the future.

SOCIAL STATICS OF
REPRESENTATIVE GOVERNMENT

Following Comte, Mill distinguishes two kinds of social science: social statics and social dynamics. The first ascertains the conditions of stability, or the causes of the persistence of a state of society. (A "state of society" is defined by the degree of knowledge and culture, the nature of the economy, the class structure, the belief system, the form of government and laws, and other prominent social facts.) Social dynamics seeks the causes

[16] *Logic*, Bk. VI, ch. X, § 8, pp. 929-30. Cumming (vol. II, pp. 365-88, 410-23) points out that Mill himself never wrote any serious work of history except (in a special sense) the *Autobiography*.

of the movement from one state of society to the next and is the province of the theory of development.[17]

Social dynamics is more fundamental than social statics. The latter states the laws of mutual interaction between the various elements within each social state, and because the "proximate cause" of each state is that state which immediately precedes it, these laws of interaction derive from the laws of social dynamics, which regulate the succession from one state to another.[18] *Representative Government* reflects this priority of social dynamics in emphasizing improvement more than stability. The theory of development and its (as yet unverified) result, the law of improvement, pervade the entire structure of Mill's argument, whereas the discussion of the conditions of stability for representative government is mainly confined to one relatively short chapter. Nevertheless, we need to consider what Mill has to say about stability because he does not prevent social dynamics from intruding into social statics. "It is . . . impossible to understand the question of the adaptation of forms of government to states of society, without taking into account not only the next step, but all the steps which society has yet to make."[19] The spirit of improvement keeps creeping into the analysis of stability.

Each of the three kinds of necessary conditions that Mill identifies determines a different degree of stability of representative democracy. First, there are the conditions that are necessary for the permanent existence of any representative government at all. Here Mill simply adapts to representative government the conditions that

---

[17] *Logic*, Bk. vi, ch. x, § 2, pp. 911-12, § 5, pp. 917-18; and *Comte*, p. 309.

[18] *Logic*, Bk. vi, ch. x, § 2, p. 912.

[19] *CRG*, ch. ii, p. 43.

he holds are necessary for the existence of any form of government. The people must be willing to accept representative government, to preserve it, especially by supporting the authorities who check the executive, and to fulfill the functions assigned to them, especially by taking an interest in public affairs and creating an effective public opinion.[20] Much of Mill's discussion of these conditions concerns how they can be developed when they do not exist—for example, how reformers might bring public opinion to favor representative government, or how even nominal representation may advance a society closer to true representative government.[21]

Second, Mill mentions some conditions that, though perhaps unnecessary for the existence of representative government, must be satisfied if it is to be preferable to other forms of government. They are principally an inclination to obey authority and a disinclination to submit to tyranny. Where a people have not yet learned the "lessons of obedience," an authoritarian ruler would be needed to maintain an adequate government. And where a people are disposed to submit to tyranny, representative government would merely result in the election of tyrannical representatives, while a strong central authority might be able to undermine the authority of local despots and thus weaken the propensity of the population to accept tyranny.[22] Here again social statics begins to dissolve into social dynamics, as Mill shows how one state of society (a stable, centralized authoritarianism) can be "instrumental in carrying the people through a necessary stage of improvement."[23]

[20] *CRG*, ch. I, pp. 6-9; ch. IV, pp. 71-72. Cf. *Logic*, Bk. VI, ch. X, § 5, pp. 920-24 (quoting "Coleridge," pp. 132-36).
[21] *CRG*, ch. IV, pp. 71, 73-74.　　[22] *CRG*, ch. IV, p. 77-79.
[23] *CRG*, ch. IV, p. 76.

Finally, there are conditions that, though their absence does not favor other forms of government, are necessary if a people are to make the best use of representative government.[24] Logically, these could embrace all the conditions that underlie a political system functioning fully in accord with Mill's theory of government, but Mill has in mind conditions that determine a more modest level of representative government. The conditions he singles out are a people's reluctance to exercise power over others and a willingness to have power exercised over themselves. England is well suited to representative government because the English people

> are very jealous of any attempt to exercise power over them, not sanctioned by long usage and by their own opinion of right; but they in general care very little for the exercise of power over others. Not having the smallest sympathy with the passion for governing, while they are but too well acquainted with the motives of private interest from which that office is sought, they prefer that it should be performed by those to whom it comes without seeking, as a consequence of social position.[25]

Mill's remarks here have been likened to the argument, made by some political scientists, that a substantial amount of apathy among citizens is necessary and desirable for a democracy.[26] The argument holds that a democratic system cannot tolerate too much participation and that it needs a cushion of political indifference to soften the impact of intensely partisan activity that

[24] *CRG*, ch. IV, p. 79.   [25] *CRG*, ch. IV, p. 84.
[26] David Y. Mayer, "John Stuart Mill and Classical Democracy," *Politics* 3 (May 1968), p. 64. Cf. the criticism by Duncan, "Mill," p. 81.

might otherwise disrupt the equilibrium of the system.[27] This is not the kind of claim Mill intends to advance, however. The nature of his objection to activism, the amount of political indifference he favors, and the remedy he proposes all differ from what is asserted by modern proponents of the argument from apathy. Mill's chief objection to the passion for governing is that it tends to multiply the number of governmental offices and to render the community insensitive to the expansion of unnecessary power. It is not an argument for political apathy or political stability per se. The problem in France, where the passion for governing prevails, is not instability but corruption, one-man dictatorship, and an oversized bureaucracy.[28] A certain amount of reluctance to rule over others is necessary—enough to prevent the excessive government that plagues France, but not so much as to inhibit the growth of participation in the properly constituted institutions of Mill's ideal representative democracy. Nothing Mill says here is inconsistent with his demands for more active participation when that participation occurs within the institutional framework outlined by his theory of government. If he approves Englishmen's "readiness to let themselves be governed by the higher classes," he does so with the understanding that the English are "determined to make their rulers always remember that they will only be governed in the way they themselves like best."[29] And even so, rule by the higher social classes is a temporary state of affairs, since the competent, to whom greater political influence should be granted, do not come mainly from the ranks of these classes. Furthermore,

---

[27] See Thompson (pp. 67-69) for citations and criticisms of this and similar views.

[28] *CRG*, ch. IV, pp. 82-83.   [29] *CRG*, ch. IV, p. 84.

the danger that greater participation might give power to the less competent can be checked by measures of civic education, including the expansion of participation. The requirements of the social statics of representative government must bend to the demands of its social dynamics.

Partly because Mill is more interested in improvement than stability, his account of the conditions for representative democracy is by modern standards incomplete and unsystematic. Robert Dahl provides one of the best recent surveys of these conditions, and many of the conditions Dahl specifies go unmentioned or unanalyzed anywhere in *Representative Government*: the precise historical sequence of competitive and inclusive political processes, access to violence and other sanctions, the structure of certain socio-economic inequalities, and various beliefs of political activists. Mill nevertheless anticipates *some* of Dahl's conditions—for example, a low degree of subcultural pluralism, freedom from domination by a foreign power, and commitment by political activists to the necessity of compromise and to the legitimacy of the political institutions.[30] A few of the other conditions on Dahl's list—a high level of socio-economic development and low levels of relative deprivation—also show up in *Representative Government*, but usually as consequences or benefits, rather than conditions, of democracy.[31]

Incomplete though Mill's analysis of the statics of democracy is, his approach to the topic is quite modern in its accent on beliefs and attitudes. Stating the conditions he typically refers to the opinions of the nation,

---

[30] Dahl, *Polyarchy*, esp. p. 203. Cf. *CRG*, ch. IV, pp. 71-72, 77-78; ch. XIII, p. 241; ch. XVI, pp. 297-98; ch. XVIII, pp. 333-36.
[31] *CRG*, ch. III, pp. 57-58, 60-61.

attachments to certain values, the state of public feel
ing, and desires and inclinations.[32] Many social scientists now similarly concentrate on beliefs and attitudes.
The longest single chapter of Dahl's *Polyarchy* is devoted
to the beliefs of activists; other writers, especially those
who study political culture, stress factors such as attitudes toward participation or toward authority.[33] However, Mill does not assemble any empirical evidence to
show that these sorts of factors are in fact the most significant for explaining stability. He evidently takes it for
granted that, if ideas are the prime cause of major social
change, as his theory of development claims, then they
are also the chief basis of stability. In still another way,
therefore, his social statics depends on his social dynamics.

GENERAL FEATURES OF DEVELOPMENT

The nature of Mill's theory of development can be
understood by examining his views on the pattern and
rate of development, its causal agency, its periods, and
the status of the laws of development. Mill has something to say about most of these topics in *Representative Government*, but the fullest exposition is to be
found in the *Logic*.[34]

Social phenomena, to a greater degree than natural
phenomena, undergo changes from one age to another,
and these changes, Mill asserts, are the result of the
mutual interaction between human character and the

[32] *CRG*, ch. IV, pp. 71-72, 78, 81-82.

[33] Almond and Verba, esp. pp. 12-26; and Harry Eckstein, *A
Theory of Stable Democracy*, Princeton, 1961.

[34] Bk. VI, chs. x-xi, pp. 911-42; also see *Comte*, pp. 263-368. The
best commentary on this aspect of his theory is by Ryan (*Mill*,
1970, pp. 169-85), on whom I rely in several parts of this section.

circumstances that shape it. Logically, such changes through time must describe either a cycle (the "recurrence of a series") or a trajectory ("a course not returning into itself"). Mill does not consider that the changes might be completely random or chaotic, conforming to no pattern at all. Nor does he present any evidence to controvert the cyclical view. He simply specifies the pattern of change as follows:

> . . . in each successive age the principal phenomena of society are different from what they were in the age preceding, and still more different from any previous age: the periods which most distinctly mark these successive changes being intervals of one generation, during which a new set of human beings have been educated, have grown up from childhood, and taken possession of society.[35]

The significance that Mill attributes to education is already apparent here, and is further underscored later by the role he assigns to ideas in the process of development. These elements in his theory of development underlie his confidence in the educative effects of participation.

Contrary to the contention of some interpreters, Mill does not subscribe to a "romantic . . . eighteenth-century Enlightenment" view of progress.[36] He does not claim to have established that the process of cumulative change or development constitutes improvement or progress in the usual sense.[37] That the general tendency

[35] *Logic*, Bk. vi, ch. x, § 3, pp. 913-14. Cf. "Michelet's History of France," in *DD*, vol. ii, p. 207; and "Guizot's Essays and Lectures on History," in *DD*, vol. ii, p. 302.

[36] Abram L. Harris, "John Stuart Mill's Theory of Progress," *Ethics* 66 (April 1956), p. 171.

[37] Mill uses "progress" or "progressive change" as equivalent

of human affairs is toward "a better and happier state" would be a "theorem" or "ultimate result" of the method he is proposing, and it cannot be finally accepted unless confirmed by the theory and evidence that this method generates.[38] In the *Logic* Mill does confess to a tentative, unsubstantiated belief in genuine progress or improvement, but in *Representative Government* he adds a further proviso:

> we ought not to forget, that there is an incessant and ever-flowing current of human affairs towards the worse, consisting of all the follies, all the vices, all the negligences, indolences, and supinenesses of mankind; which is only controlled, and kept from sweeping all before it, by the exertions which some persons constantly, and others by fits, put forth in the direction of good and worthy objects. . . . A very small diminution of those exertions would not only put a stop to improvement, but would turn the general tendency of things towards deterioration; which, once begun, would proceed with increasing rapidity, and become more and more difficult to check, until it reached a state often seen in history, and in which many large portions of mankind even now grovel. . . .[39]

Through this distinctly Manichean synthesis Mill combines the classical theme of degeneration (noted earlier

---

to "cumulative change," which does not necessarily imply improvement, i.e., progress in the ordinary sense (*Logic*, Bk. IV, ch. X, § 3, pp. 913-14).

[38] The term "theorem" is in the final text, whereas "ultimate result" appears in the original manuscript and the first two editions (*Logic*, p. 914, note ff).

[39] *CRG*, ch. II, pp. 26-27. Cf. "To Charles A. Cummings" (Feb. 23, 1863), *Later Letters*, in *CW*, vol. XV, pp. 842-44.

in Rousseau's theory of history) with the theme of improvement through human effort.[40] It is perhaps an unstable mixture, but it hardly justifies ascribing a high degree of optimism to Mill.

Because of the perpetual threat of deterioration, efforts toward improvement must be gradual. Mill distrusts massive changes or revolutionary reforms not only because they often involve violence (to which he strongly objects[41]) but also because, in the face of the "current . . . towards the worse," they create a risk of forfeiting what has already been achieved. This is not to say that revolutions are never justified; they are if there is no other way to initiate necessary improvements.[42] Mill expresses considerable sympathy for radical socialist schemes that would organize workers into cooperatives, collectively owning their means of production. But unlike Marx, Mill prefers the method of the utopian socialists, who would set up model communities to show whether socialism can succeed, rather than the strategy of the revolutionary socialists, who would remake society before anyone knows whether socialism can work at all.[43] Revolutionaries would jeopardize the benefits of the present level of development. Generally, Mill recommends piecemeal reforms (such as most of those in

[40] Manicheanism is the only form of belief in the supernatural that Mill thinks is "wholly clear both of intellectual contradiction and of moral obliquity"; it may be held in conjunction with (though not as a substitute for) the Religion of Humanity (*Three Essays on Religion* ["Utility of Religion"], pp. 425-26).

[41] "Notes on the Newspapers," *Monthly Repository* 8 (April 1834), pp. 311-12; and "Chapters on Socialism," pp. 737, 749.

[42] "A Few Observations on the French Revolution," in *DD*, vol. I, p. 85.

[43] *Political Economy*, Bk. II, ch. i, § 4, pp. 210-14; and "Chapters on Socialism," pp. 745-46.

Representative Government), which, though intended to have radical consequences in the future, do not immediately require any sharp break with the social structures, values, and beliefs existing at present. For this reason the principles of participation and competence, and the reduction of the tension between them, cannot be implemented fully or all at once. Even if the principles did not have to be traded off against each other, we would still have to proceed gradually in promoting each one separately so that those aspects of each that have already been realized would not be lost.[44]

The "prime causal agent" that impels development or maintains its current level against the forces of retrogression is the "state of speculative faculties of mankind; including the nature of the beliefs which by any means they arrived at, concerning themselves and the world by which they are surrounded."[45] Mill does not suppose that most people are motivated by a yearning for knowledge; on the contrary, the strongest motive for improvement is the desire for increased material comfort. But the technological advances that would satisfy this desire depend on the state of knowledge at any time. Similarly, improvements in social organization require that the more powerful propensities of human nature (those "which partake most of the nature of selfishness") be subordinated to a set of shared values. By this route "the state of the speculative faculties . . .

---

[44] It is therefore a misreading to ascribe to Mill, as Karl Popper does in *The Poverty of Historicism* (New York, 1960, pp. 72-73), the doctrine of "holism"—at least in any form that denies the possibility of piecemeal and gradual reform. See Ryan, *Mill*, 1970, p. 181.

[45] *Logic*, Bk. vi, ch. x, § 7, pp. 925-26. Cf. *CRG*, ch. i, pp. 13-14, and *Comte*, pp. 315-17.

actually determines the moral and political state of community."[46]

As they stand, these propositions may look tautologous, stating only that men will not do what they do not know how to do.[47] But the propositions must be understood as only preliminary indications of what a theory of development, coupled with a science of human character ("ethology"), might eventually formulate and establish.[48] The propositions that such a theory puts forward would have to be refined and tested by the "general facts of history," some of which Mill offers as examples of the kind of evidence for which one would look to establish that intellectual factors are the prime agency of development. Every considerable change in human affairs, Mill thinks, has been preceded by a change in the state of knowledge, which in turn had for its precursor the previous states of belief and thought.[49] In *Representative Government* he illustrates the efficacy of ideas by alluding to religious leaders, such as Christ and Luther, whose beliefs made them more influential than their opponents, and to the European rulers of the last half of the eighteenth century whose liberal and reformist ideas eventually undermined their own absolute authority. He also mentions the demise of Negro slavery and the emancipation of the Russian serfs, which both followed a "spread of moral convictions" and "the growth of more enlightened opinion respecting the true interest of the State." Indeed, it is by the spread of ideas, such as those contained in *Repre-*

[46] *Logic*, ch. x, § 7, pp. 925-26.
[47] Ryan, *Mill*, 1970, p. 178.
[48] *Logic*, Bk. vi, ch. v, pp. 861-74. Mill enthusiastically advocates ethology but never really begins to construct even the rudiments of such a science.
[49] *Logic*, Bk. vi, ch. x, § 7, pp. 926-27.

sentative Government itself, that the realization of the principles of participation and competence will be promoted.[50]

Although Mill does not believe that he has done more than *suggest* that ideas are the chief causal agent of development, he apparently does not see any objection in principle to the project of establishing this conclusion. A major problem besetting any single-factor account of historical development, whether Mill's or others like Marx's, is the difficulty of distinguishing the effects of the allegedly prime factor from the effects of other factors. Temporal priority is not a sufficient criterion, since there are almost always other factors that are also temporally prior. Mill earlier in the *Logic* mentions something like this difficulty, but he proceeds with his discussion of a prime causal agent as if the difficulty were of no consequence.[51]

Even if we could isolate the various factors in development, it is not clear on what basis we could decide which is the prime one. Had Mill read Marx, he would have found a completely contrary view of development, for Marx maintains that economic factors (more specifically, the mode of production in material life) determine the "general character of the social, political and spiritual processes of life." Marx writes that "it is not the consciousness of men that determines their existence but, on the contrary, their social existence determines their consciousness." The ideas, or the "state of intellectual faculties," are merely the "superstructure" or the "ideological forms" in which men fight out the underlying economic conflicts that propel society from one stage to

[50] *CRG*, ch. I, pp. 13-16; and Preface, pp. v-vi. Cf. *Liberty*, ch. II, p. 63; and "A Few Observations. . . ," p. 83.
[51] *Logic*, Bk. VI, ch. X, § 6, p. 924.

the next.[52] Mill of course was not unaware of views that assert the primacy of material or economic factors; his argument in *Representative Government* for the power of ideas is in part directed against such views.[53] But compared to Marx's theory, the notions Mill criticizes are crude. Although Marx's theory is not free of difficulties (he shares with Mill, for example, the problems that confound single-factor theories), it is a more elaborate and challenging theory of development than any of those against which Mill argues.[54] If Mill had been familiar with it, he might have been provoked to work out his own view of the primacy of ideas beyond the merely sketchy beginnings he offered. Even so, any such project would have eventually become mired in the conceptual difficulties we have noticed.

Mill's belief in the primacy of ideas also influences his scheme for distinguishing periods in the process of development. No longer is Mill content with characterizing periods in terms of order and progress, as he was earlier.[55] The distinction between order and prog-

[52] Marx, *A Contribution to the Critique of Political Economy*, ed. Maurice Dobb, tr. S. W. Ryazanskaya, New York, 1970, pp. 20-21. Also cf. Marx and Engels, *The German Ideology*, ed. R. Pascal, New York, 1947, esp. pp. 16-43; and *The Holy Family*, tr. R. Dixon, Moscow, 1956, esp. p. 254.

[53] *CRG*, ch. II, pp. 14-15.

[54] Mill shares with Marx another general problem—that of reconciling the aim of a determinist social science or theory of history with an activist view of social and political reform. Mill's attempts to resolve this conflict are in the *Logic*, Bk. VI, ch. ii, pp. 836-43, and ch. xi, §§ 2-4, pp. 934-42.

[55] The earlier division, inspired by the Saint-Simonians, is most clearly presented in the "Spirit of the Age." In the *Logic* Mill praises Comte's scheme, which distinguished periods according to the bases for claims to knowledge dominant in each period (theological, metaphysical, and positive or scientific), but Mill thinks that Comte's theory is not very useful for predicting the future (*Logic*, Bk. VI, ch. x, § 8, pp. 928-29).

ress that he finds least unsatisfactory is that the former preserves goods already existing, whereas the latter seeks to increase them. But he rejects even this distinction as a basis for a "philosophy of government"—and for reasons that apply equally to a theory of development: "the agencies which tend to preserve the social good which already exists, are the very same which promote the increase of it, and *vice versa*. . . ."[56] Instead, Mill distinguishes periods of development—usually implicitly—according to which power in society is in ascent at any particular time; these powers include at various times spiritual and temporal authorities, military, territorial, or industrial classes, and the numerical majority, which is dominant in the present age.[57] The dominant power bears the ideas that determine the general character of the age or generation, but development or improvement occurs only if the ideas of the dominant power are challenged by rival powers, at least one of which evidently embodies what will be the prepotent idea of the next period. Without such challenges, stagnation and then decay ensue.[58] These ominous prospects underscore the crucial importance of the competent minority in democratic institutions. Without a "rallying point, for opinions which the ascendant public opinion views with disfavour," the process of development is not likely to lead to improvement.[59] But we should also add, in the spirit of Mill's theory, that increased participation can similarly contribute to the process of improvement. By extending the range of opinions expressed in the political system, participation diversifies "ascendant public opin-

[56] *CRG*, ch. II, p. 21.
[57] *CRG*, ch. VII, p. 149.
[58] *CRG*, ch. VII, p. 149; also, ch. II, p. 42. Cf. *Liberty*, ch. III, esp. pp. 130-33; and "Guizot," pp. 316-18.
[59] *CRG*, ch. VII, p. 150.

ion" and thus creates additional challenges to prevailing views.

Theories of development (and the social sciences), Mill believes, have a long way to go before they can offer truly scientific laws that would explain each of the "leading circumstances" of one period by reference to its causes in the preceding period. The proper method for the social and historical sciences is inverse deduction, which calls for at least three ingredients: laws of human nature; middle-level principles (*axiomata media*) that indicate how one social state generates another; and empirical generalizations that characterize past trends. Ideally, the generalizations give rise to middle-level principles, which in turn are verified by being deduced from, or shown to be consistent with, laws of human nature (though Mill concedes that these connections are not always strictly deductive).[60]

So far we not only lack the science of human character that would supply the laws of human nature, but we also do not even have the necessary middle-level principles. All that social science as yet offers are generalizations about tendencies in the past. Mill terms these "empirical laws," but this is a misleading designation, since they are not strictly speaking laws at all but merely statements of "what is common to large classes of observed facts."[61] Despite his terminology, Mill acknowledges the difference between genuine laws and trends, thus escaping Karl Popper's criticism of the "historicists" who ignore the difference. However, Popper accuses Mill, along with other historicists, of overlooking the "dependence of trends on initial conditions." Accord-

[60] *Logic*, Bk. vi, ch. ix, § 4, pp. 915-17.
[61] *Logic*, Bk. vi, ch. ix, § 5, p. 907.

ing to Popper, Mill believes that his favorite trends will continue indefinitely into the future, and thus puts forward prophecies instead of predictions. But Mill insists that his "empirical laws" or trends do presuppose initial conditions or "remoter causes" (as well as the laws of ethology and psychology).[62] With this view Popper has no quarrel, though he mistakenly believes that it is not Mill's. Popper's criticism is further defused by his approval of Mill's method of inverse deduction, which Popper considers proper procedure for social as well as natural science.[63] Moreover, Mill's "deep sense of uncertainty" about any prediction based on trends or generalizations undermines Popper's attempt to cast him in the role of a historicist prophet.[64] Besides the uncertainty about changes in the initial conditions, the impact of the remarkable individual will also disturb our predictions (at least predictions about the rate at which development occurs).[65] Nevertheless, Mill urges that we study current trends and encourage those that are "salutary" while trying to counteract those that are "hurtful."[66] Following his own suggestion, Mill in *Representative Government* and other writings, identifies a number of trends that tentatively support his recommendations for promoting the principle of participation and the principle of competence over time.

[62] Popper, pp. 120-21, 128-30; and *Logic*, Bk. vi, ch. ix, § 6, p. 908. Cf. Ryan, *Mill*, 1970, pp. 182-83.

[63] Popper, pp. 128, 121.

[64] "Tocqueville," in *DD*, p. 140; and *Logic*, Bk. vi, ch. ix, § 6, pp. 909-10.

[65] *Logic*, Bk. vi, ch. xi, § 3, pp. 938-39.

[66] "Tocqueville," in *DD*, p. 140. Unlike Tocqueville, Comte failed in these tasks, according to Mill, because he did not relate his predictions and prescriptions to the laws of development (*Comte*, p. 325).

THE TREND TOWARD EQUALITY

The most significant trend in recent history, according to Mill, is the increasing tendency toward equality in all spheres of social and political life. Differences among individuals in various classes, occupations, and regions are gradually disappearing, as people read the same publications, attend similar schools, and exercise the same political rights. The more that people become alike, the more the power of the mass or the numerical majority grows to overwhelm that of the individual or the competent few.[67] These tendencies give rise to social tyranny or conformity, which Mill seeks to counter, in the first instance, by means of institutions that help realize the principle of competence. Generally, Mill stresses the adverse more than the auspicious consequences of equality—evidently because he feels that the latter will come about with little effort, whereas the former can be prevented only by deliberate design. Most interpreters of Mill, therefore, concentrate almost exclusively on his mistrust of social equality. If, however, the undesirable consequences of equality that we examined in Chapter 2 were its only results, Mill would have little reason to hope that representative government could overcome its "natural tendency towards collective mediocrity," let alone to believe that representative government could advance in the future. The fruits of greater equality are not all baneful since some of them support the educative effects of participation, which stimulate the improvement of representative democracy.

Representative Government depicts at least three

[67] *CRG*, ch. VII, pp. 148-50; *Liberty*, ch. III, pp. 130-32; and *Logic*, Bk. VI, ch. X, § 6, pp. 924-25.

favorable aspects of the trend toward equality. First, although equality may go too far in undermining the "reverential spirit," that it "destroys reverence for mere social position must be counted among the good . . . part of its influences."[68] Relying less on social status as a guide for choosing leaders, citizens are forced to form their judgments on more substantial grounds, and consequently their participation is more likely to advance their political education. Second, the "increasing emphasis, pronouncing against the claim of society to decide for individuals what they are and are not fit for, and what they shall and shall not be allowed to attempt" similarly enhances the likelihood that all citizens equally will be able to make political decisions more often on their own.[69] Expanding upon this idea in *The Subjection of Women*, Mill suggests that in earlier periods of history, social morality was characterized by obligations to submit to power; then arose the right of the weaker members of society to have protection. We are now entering an era of

> sympathetic association; having its root no longer in the instinct of equals for self-protection, but in a cultivated sympathy between them; and no one being now left out, but an equal measure being extended to all. . . . [T]he true virtue of human beings is fitness to live together as equals; claiming nothing for themselves but what they as freely concede to every one else; regarding command of any kind as an exceptional necessity, and in all cases a temporary one; and preferring, whenever possible, the society of those with whom leading and following can be alternate and reciprocal.[70]

[68] *CRG*, ch. XII, pp. 231-32.   [69] *CRG*, ch. VIII, p. 184.
[70] *Subjection of Women*, ch. II, pp. 80-81.

As a third consequence of equality Mill expects that poverty, at least its extreme forms, will gradually diminish.[71] This development should expand the electorate and (though Mill does not say so explicitly) should also reduce somewhat the gross inequalities in political resources that hamper extensive participation.

Some of Mill's other writings limn broader trends that support the improvement of representative democracy. Reviewing Tocqueville's work, Mill points to the "diffusion of intelligence" that is associated with the increasing equality in America. This intellectual improvement is partly an effect of democracy, as Tocqueville argues, but it is also, Mill thinks, partly a consequence of broader causes, such as the prior education and habits of Americans, which reinforce the trend toward equality and democracy.[72] More equal educational opportunities thus should continue to raise the quality of participation in the future, just as participation itself promotes civic education. "Advancing civilisation" will also strengthen and extend moral competence, or the concern for the general interest, though not, as Comte thought, to the point of eliminating self-interested passions.[73] One source of this improvement is accumulated experience. The principle of utility, on which our judgments of the general interest ultimately rest, must be applied by means of "secondary principles" that, like "the precepts of every practical art, admit of indefinite improvement." Societies have learned and will continue to learn how to refine and strengthen these principles.[74] Mill in this way shows more respect

[71] *CRG*, ch. VIII, p. 173.
[72] "Tocqueville," in *DD*, p. 105.
[73] *Comte*, p. 339.
[74] *Utilitarianism*, ch. II, p. 224; but cf. *Liberty*, ch. II, pp. 65-67.

for custom and tradition in framing moral principles than does Bentham, who often writes as if a new utilitarian moral code could spring full-blown from the minds of one generation of philosophers.[75] We certainly should challenge traditional principles, Mill believes, but so that we do not lose the gains that previous generations have achieved, we must proceed cautiously. Our chances of improving on tradition are enhanced by the very fact that it already contains much of value.

Another foundation for moral improvement comes from "removing the sources of opposition of interest, and levelling those inequalities of legal privilege between individuals and classes, owing to which there are large portions of mankind whose happiness it is still practicable to disregard." The growing importance of equal association and cooperation, making citizens more dependent on one another, encourages them to identify their purposes with the purposes of others.[76] Later Mill recognizes that this "same progress makes society and its interests more complicated" and that "greater compass and elevation of mind become necessary for comprehending them."[77] But he still affirms that the diffusion of intelligence and public spirit can cope with the consequences of the increased complexity of modern society.

Trends in the economy reinforce the other trends contributing toward the improvement of representative democracy. Because of the spread of egalitarian

[75] "Bentham," pp. 89-91; and *Comte*, p. 325.

[76] *Utilitarianism*, ch. III, pp. 231-32.

[77] "Centralisation," p. 336. In this passage Mill is summarizing the views of Dupont-White, but he himself apparently accepts this part of the argument, denying only that the increased complexity requires a proportionate increase in the activities of government (pp. 346-48).

161

ideas (ideas remain the prime causal agent), the division between employers and employees cannot be permanently maintained, and economic institutions will become increasingly cooperative. Society eventually may even be ready for socialism. But whether or not socialism is the wave of the future, class conflict will diminish, allaying the urgency of maintaining bulwarks against incompetence and majority tyranny. Burgeoning prosperity, along with technological and scientific advances, will give individuals more control over their lives.[78] All of these circumstances tend to raise the competence of all citizens and enhance their ability to participate effectively in politics.

Mill does not rely on indefinite growth in the economy to sustain these trends, however. Following Ricardo, he holds that the economy will ultimately settle into a stationary state because a declining rate of profit will discourage capital investment, while population increases (which must be restrained even to maintain the stationary state) will absorb any real gains in productivity. Mill's prediction of a stationary state rests on *a priori* theory rather than on careful analysis of empirical data. Had he examined the actual economic trends of the first half of his century, he would have seen that although population nearly doubled, the national product (in constant prices) had more than kept pace with it, and that output and investment were increasing in key industries.[79]

[78] *Political Economy*, Bk. IV, ch. vii, §§ 4-5, pp. 766-77, 769-75; Preface, p. xciii; ch. i, §§ 1-2, pp. 705-9; "Chapters on Socialism," pp. 745-46, 750; and *Comte*, p. 312. On Mill's attitude toward socialism, see Robson, pp. 245-71, and Pedro Schwartz, *The New Political Economy of J. S. Mill*, Durham, N.C., 1972, pp. 153-92.

[79] *Political Economy*, Bk. IV, ch. iv, § 4, pp. 738-41; Bk. II,

Mill is not unhappy about the prospect of a stationary economy because he envisions a state with

> these leading features: a well-paid and affluent body of labourers; no enormous fortunes, except what were earned and accumulated during a single lifetime; but a much larger body of persons than at present, not only exempt from the coarser toils, but with sufficient leisure, both physical and mental, from mechanical details, to cultivate freely the graces of life, and afford examples of them to the classes less favourably circumstanced for their growth.[80]

Here Mill forsakes Ricardo for the Saint-Simonians. He welcomes the end of the "struggling to get on; that trampling, crushing, elbowing, and treading on each other's heels" that characterize the necessary but brutal early phases of economic progress.[81] Though economically stationary, society will continue to improve in other respects. Individuals will be free to concentrate on inventing labor-saving techniques, discovering more noble incentives than the "cruder stimuli" of economic competition, and creating a more equitable distribution of wealth (for example, by prohibiting the inheritance of wealth).[82] The active, achieving type of character will

---

ch. xi, § 3, pp. 343-46; Bk. I, ch. xiii, § 2, p. 190; Holthoon, pp. 146-47; and Philip Deane and W. A. Cole, *British Economic Growth, 1688-1959*, Cambridge, Eng., 1964, pp. 213, 216, 225, 263, 266. For Mill's debt to Ricardo and a general critique of his economic thought, see Schwartz, esp. pp. 7-21, 61-66, 208-12; and Holthoon, esp. pp. 135-73.

[80] *Political Economy*, Bk. IV, ch. vi, § 2, p. 755.

[81] *Political Economy*, Bk. IV, ch. vi, § 2, p. 754.

[82] *Political Economy*, Bk. v, ch. ix, § 2, p. 891; Bk. IV, ch. vi, § 2, pp. 754-57.

not vanish from the scene, but he will direct his energy toward more humane pursuits.

If Mill's account of the trend toward equality is approximately correct, many of the very same tendencies that induce him to stress the importance of competent leadership also provide a basis for a wider diffusion of competence among all citizens. Insofar as competence becomes more widely realized, participation can become more extensive with less loss of competence. Over time the conflict between the principles of competence and participation would in this way diminish. Moreover, as competence spreads further, participation is more likely, through its educative effects, to raise the level of competence still more. Participation and competence thus will mutually reinforce each other. Since the underlying tendency toward equality has its untoward aspects, the need for the influence of competent leaders will not completely disappear. But if the favorable trends are reinforced and the negative trends dampened by efforts of reform, the principles of both participation and competence could be more nearly effected in the future. The theory of development points toward this possibility and suggests how it might be realized.

Taken in its most general terms, Mill's projection of a trend toward equality has considerable validity. Compared to the governments of his time, modern democracies provide citizens with greater social and political rights, a higher standard of living, more leisure, and better educational opportunities. The extension of these benefits to more and more citizens during the past hundred years or so has been chronicled by T. H. Marshall, who describes the process as a growth of citizenship or "basic human equality"—the fundamental rights due to individuals by virtue of their membership in a state. Citizenship has broadened from civil rights (which mainly secure individual liberty) to political rights (which support political participation) and finally in the twentieth century to social rights (which guarantee a certain level of economic well-being). Indeed, the expansion of social rights may have gone further than Mill expected or perhaps even desired, leading to greater paternalism than he would have tolerated.[83]

Many of the features that appear in Mill's projections find their way into the portrait of post-industrial society presented by some social scientists in recent years. Of the six characteristics that, according to a recent analysis, define the concept of a post-industrial society, Mill anticipates four: a high degree of affluence and well-being; high levels of education; a value structure more concerned with the quality of life than with material achievement; and a central role for knowledge and technology.[84] (Mill does not mention the predominance of the service sector in the economy and white-collar workers in the labor force—the two other characteristics ascribed to post-industrial society.) Since Comte, who greatly influenced Mill's theory of development, is sometimes cited as a precursor of theories of post-industrial society, Mill's projections naturally adumbrate certain aspects of those theories. But other aspects so transgress Mill's theory that he should be counted as much a critic

[83] T. H. Marshall, *Class, Citizenship and Social Development*, New York, 1964, pp. 71-134; and *Social Policy in the 20th Century*, 3d ed., London, 1970, pp. 17-18.

[84] Samuel P. Huntington, "Postindustrial Politics: How Benign Will it Be?" *Comparative Politics* 6 (Jan. 1974), pp. 163-64. Cf. Daniel Bell, *The Coming of Post-Industrial Society*, New York, 1973, pp. 12-13, 114-15; and Zbigniew Brzezinski, *Between Two Ages*, New York, 1970, pp. 10-14. For an analysis that substantiates many of these trends but also insists on the possibility of increasing political participation, see Inglehart, esp. chs. 2-3, 10.

as an advocate of the idea of post-industrial society. Just as he decried the elitism of Comte's theory, so he surely would not accept the only slightly less extreme elitism that pervades some modern theories of post-industrial society. Neither Comte's highly trained, opulent elite who make up the "temporal power" that rules the economy and the state nor their modern analogues in post-industrial society—the technocratic elite—are sufficiently accountable to satisfy Mill's theory of democracy.[85]

Another feature of some theories of post-industrial society would disconcert Mill. With Mill, some of these theorists foresee the continued growth of political participation, and even a decline in the importance of large political parties, but whereas Mill would welcome these developments, these theorists deprecate them. Samuel Huntington, for example, suggests that increased participation is likely to make post-industrial society more difficult to govern: ". . . widespread education tends to produce too much interest and participation which leads in turn to political stalemate. Innovation is easier when substantial portions of the population are indifferent."[86] This appears to be simply a more sophisticated version of the argument from apathy. Although Mill does not explicitly consider the argument in this guise, his hope plainly is that as citizens become more competent, they will also see the need to cooperate in order to achieve innovative social goals and will be willing to accept leadership that moves in this direction. Whether this hope can be sustained depends less on the recent experience of modern democracies than on the ultimate validity of Mill's case for the educative effects of participation.

[85] *Comte*, pp. 347-51.
[86] Huntington, "Postindustrial," pp. 172-77.

The broad egalitarian drift of development in modern times, projected by Mill, is admitted by social scientists, but the precise nature and consequences of that trend remain controversial matters, and in a number of respects Mill's views of this process must be considerably qualified. Indeed, the qualifications that must be attached to any statement of a trend toward equality almost overwhelm the statement itself. During the 1950s and early 1960s many social scientists believed that society was rapidly approaching the harmonious state that Mill hoped eventually would be achieved. They claimed that class differences were becoming less sharp, the barriers between classes less formidable, and class and ideological conflict less pronounced.[87] More recently, however, significant limitations on the trend toward equality have been noted. The growth of citizenship or basic human equality is, as Marshall recognized, quite compatible with the persistence of marked inequality, especially in the class structure.[88]

Equality has stopped short of any radical redistribution of income and wealth in modern democracies, and the relative positions of various classes in modern society have changed little, at least in the past thirty years. Economic growth evidently begets greater social equality but only up to a certain point, after which inequality may actually increase.[89] Nor has the general rise in

[87] S. M. Lipset, *Political Man*, New York, 1963, p. 403; Raymond Aron, *Progress and Disillusion*, New York, 1968; and cf. Mostafa Rejai (ed.), *Decline of Ideology?* Chicago, 1971. This is also the view of some of the writers who proclaim the advent of a post-industrial society.

[88] Marshall, *Class*, pp. 94-95, 101, 112-15, 128.

[89] Jackman, p. 198; Charles Anderson, *The Political Economy of Social Class*, Englewood Cliffs, N.J., 1974, pp. 93-94, 111-15; Simon Kuznets, "Income Distribution and Changes in Consumption," in Hoke S. Simpson (ed.), *The Changing American Population*, New

prosperity eradicated poverty in modern democracies. Mill was not blind to the possibility that while "many of the poor might grow rich," the "class at the base of the whole might increase in numbers only and not in comfort nor in cultivation."[90] But he probably would have been surprised to see the pockets of poverty that persist in a society as prosperous as the United States.[91] Furthermore, despite the real expansion of educational opportunities since Mill's time, access to superior education is still significantly determined by class origins.[92] Partly as a consequence of this bias, opportunities for better occupations and for the exercise of political influence are far from equal.[93]

To the extent that class conflict has become less severe, it is largely because of the rapid growth of national income.[94] By doubting the possibility of continued eco-

---

York, 1962, esp. p. 30; R. M. Titmuss, *Income Distribution and Social Change*, London, 1962, esp. pp. 36-53; and Sidney Pollard and David W. Crossley, *The Wealth of Britain, 1085-1966*, London, 1968, pp. 257-66.

[90] *Political Economy*, Bk. iv, ch. i, § 2, p. 709.

[91] See Stanley Lebergott, *Wealth and Want*, Princeton, 1976; Bradley Schiller, *The Economics of Poverty and Discrimination*, Englewood Cliffs, N.J., 1973, pp. 20, 25-28; and Alan B. Batchelder, *The Economics of Poverty*, 2d ed., New York, 1971, p. 62.

[92] T. B. Bottomore, *Classes in Modern Society*, New York, 1966, pp. 45-46; "The Class Structure in Western Europe," in Margaret Archer and Salvador Giner (eds.), *Contemporary Europe*, London, 1971, p. 401; James Littlejohn, *Social Stratification*, London, 1972, pp. 121-28; and Samuel Bowles and Herbert Gintis, *Schooling in Capitalist America*, New York, 1976, pp. 26-36.

[93] Seymour Martin Lipset and Reinhard Bendix, *Social Mobility in Industrial Society*, Berkeley, 1959, pp. 94-96; Peter M. Blau and Otis Dudley Duncan, *The American Occupational Structure*, New York, 1967, pp. 402-3, 425. For the effects on participation, see Thompson, pp. 168-72.

[94] Bottomore, *Classes*, p. 42. Cf. Inglehart, ch. 7.

nomic growth, Mill disparaged what turned out to be a chief source of the reduction of conflict between groups. It must be said, however, that Mill would not have regarded the present resolution of conflict as genuine and permanent, concealing as it does profound divisions among social classes and lacking the basis for all groups in society to cooperate in pursuit of a general interest. And in such measure as social concord depends on continued economic growth, the social and cultural costs of such growth would have further detracted from any satisfaction Mill might have felt, had he been able to witness the later eclipse of conflict. A number of modern economists and social critics today reaffirm his strictures on economic growth.[95]

Besides economic growth, a major cause of changes in the relations between classes has been the relative shift in the occupational structure of modern societies from blue-collar and manufacturing to white-collar and service positions.[96] Mill predicted that growing numbers of the working class would become middle class in certain respects, but he seemed to think that this would be a consequence of increases in the rate of mobility per se rather than of changes in the occupational structure.[97]

[95] See Dennis L. Meadows et al., *The Limits of Growth*, New York, 1972; and Mancur Olson and Hans H. Landsberg (eds.), *The No-Growth Society*, New York, 1973. Mill figures prominently in a newspaper editorial questioning the desirability of growth ("Learning From Error," *New York Times*, Aug. 12, 1972, p. 22).

[96] Cf. Lipset and Bendix, pp. 13-28, 83-91, 108-9; Blau and Duncan, pp. 23-28, 103, 105, 424, 429; and Constance Serrentino, "Comparing Employment Shifts in 10 Industrialized Countries," *Monthly Labor Review* 94 (Oct. 1971), p. 6.

[97] "Tocqueville," in *DD*, pp. 98-99. Mill assumes only that the working class will become "well paid, well taught, and well conducted" (*ibid.*), not that they will necessarily become middle class in their style of life, their status aspirations, or their po-

A significant expansion of the middle class has indeed occurred, and the number of opportunities for higher status are therefore greater. If this trend continues, it could reduce disparities in education, income, occupation, and ultimately in the exercise of political influence and participation. But what seems more likely is that the trend will simply raise the absolute level of these benefits, leaving the relative inequalities in the benefits intact. The contours of these alternative courses remain vague and unexplored in Mill's sociology.

That all forms of class conflict will vanish, even with further equality, is doubtful. There are plenty of sources of potential conflict that are not likely to disappear, though the lines of battle may be drawn differently in the future. The growing discrepancies between the conditions that citizens encounter at work and at leisure could generate acute discontent and lead to further demands for, among other things, more worker control over decisions in industry. Tensions are also likely to grow between declining groups such as blue-collar workers and central city residents, on the one hand, and rising groups such as white-collar workers and suburban residents, on the other; employees in public and private sectors of the economy, too, are likely to find their interests increasingly in opposition.[98] We may be just beginning to move into the period of social strife that Mill in his

---

litical attitudes. Hence, his view should not be identified with the *embourgeoisement* thesis that has been called into question, e.g., by John H. Goldthorpe et al., *The Affluent Worker in the Class Structure*, Cambridge, Eng., 1969, pp. 157-95.

[98] Bottomore, *Classes*, pp. 97-98; Huntington, "Postindustrial," pp. 177-82; Anthony Giddens, *The Class Structure of the Advanced Societies*, London, 1973, pp. 282-87, 292-93; and Alford, pp. 309-41. Cf. Duncan, *Marx and Mill*, pp. 300-11.

time saw immediately ahead, rather than into the period of social tranquility that he deemed more remote.

Insofar as the trend toward equality stops short of Mill's expectations, the resolution of the conflict between competence and participation will prove more difficult than he hoped. The extension of what Marshall calls citizenship certainly helps, but the remaining social inequalities impede the diffusion of competence and the further growth of participation. Yet Mill never believed that the trends toward equality would by themselves generate the necessary improvement in representative democracy. They could not do so because, first, the problems occasioned by greater equality are at least as great as its benefits and, second, if the benign face of equality is to be appreciated, social and political reforms, deliberately designed to reinforce this aspect of equality and to dampen its pernicious aspect, must be implemented. The course of human development must in any case always struggle against the pervasive forces of stagnancy and decay.

It is not surprising that Mill was partly mistaken about the precise nature and consequences of the trend toward equality. He was himself skeptical of long-range predictions, and even more doubtful of their validity when offered, as they were by him and by later social scientists, without the foundation that a thoroughgoing theory of development would provide. Most of the projections of contemporary social science are based mainly on trends and correlations that have obtained in recent years, and some of these are already beginning to change significantly.[99] These changes underscore Mill's warning to treat with caution any prediction based simply on

[99] Cf. Huntington, "Postindustrial," pp. 190-91.

171

"empirical laws" or extrapolations from past correlations rather than on genuine scientific laws that a theory of development would propound. Furthermore, when social scientists move from data to broader interpretations, their views become controversial and, as we have noticed, tend to fluctuate from generation to generation. It cannot be said, therefore, that we now possess, as a means of assessing Mill's account of equality, a theory that is widely accepted by social scientists, or that is likely to be so accepted in the future.

Today Mill's theory of development would be classed with "speculative" philosophies of history, which seek a pattern of meaning in history beyond the professional concern of the ordinary historian. Contrary to Mill's expectations, this kind of theory or philosophy has become increasingly rare, and less respectable, as the standards for the acceptance of historical fact have risen and as the study of history has become more specialized.[100] Speculation, often more lax than Mill's, abounds in recent social science but rarely in conjunction with comprehensive and systematic theorizing. More rigorous conceptions of social and historical science that Mill himself encouraged have made it more difficult to construct the grand social theories that he also promoted. The concern for rigor has evoked a reluctance to raise in systematic theory the larger questions that vexed Mill—such as whether development tends toward improvement. Mill's own endeavors toward a theory of development suffer from serious methodological flaws, and many of his substantive "laws" and predictions are,

---

[100] William H. Dray, *Philosophy of History*, Englewood Cliffs, N.J., 1964, pp. 1, 61. Mill's reasons for believing that a theory of development would become increasingly feasible are given in the *Logic*, Bk. vi, ch. xi, § 4, p. 942.

to say the least, questionable. But he clearly shows—what many social scientists and theorists ignore—that a theory of democracy needs a theory of development. A satisfactory theory of democracy relies on some kind of theory of development to provide a critical standard for challenging democracies existing at any time and to serve as a guide for improving democracies in the future.

Conclusion

Now that the major components of Mill's theory of democracy have been explored, the structure of that theory can be better appreciated. This chapter reviews the structure of the theory and its relation to recent social science and democratic theory. At the same time it presents some criticisms of basic features of the theory and suggests some modifications that could meet these criticisms. If Mill's theory, even when amended, is not wholly satisfactory, it nevertheless stands, after more than a century, as a valuable source for contemporary theorizing about democracy.

THE STRUCTURE OF MILL'S THEORY

The structure of Mill's theory of democracy follows the pattern suggested by his two criteria for the "goodness of government"—how well a government uses the qualities that exist at any particular time in a polity, and how well a government contributes to the improvement of those qualities in the future. In the justifications for the principles of participation and competence, the first criterion takes the form of a protective argument for each principle, and the second criterion appears as an educative argument for each.

The protective argument for participation seeks to show that all the major interests that citizens wish to express should have a voice in the political process; among the various consequences of this claim are that members of the working class should hold seats in Parliament, and that citizens should consider political issues in choosing representatives. This argument, however, is not sufficient to establish that real interests or the general interest will be reliably effected through participation, and Mill therefore needs the educative argument, which is supposed to show that participation promotes an ideal type of national character, manifested in an active and public-spirited citizenry.

The protective argument for competence indicates the need for leadership by better qualified citizens to guard against instrumental and moral incompetence both in the government and in the public (especially majority tyranny). But competent leaders do not merely cautiously protect the existing good qualities in government. Assuming the role of political educators, they strive to strengthen the civic capacities of all citizens and, to the extent that they are successful, render their protective role redundant.

At any given time the two principles come together in Mill's theory of government, which, like Aristotle's idea of mixed government, stipulates that both the principles be recognized in each of the major political institutions. The design of each institution is intended to give the principles equivalent scope for being realized. The balance between the two principles, however, never hangs exactly even, and the theory of government leaves a great deal of room for working out in practice the relative shares of influence that the principles exercise over the operation of the various institutions.

Like Mill's social statics, the theory of government

views the conditions for sustaining government as a cross-section of history at some particular time, though unlike the social statics, the theory prescribes conditions for a particular form of government, and these conditions go beyond those that are necessary only for the stability of the government. Mill's social dynamics and his theory of development are more closely parallel. The social dynamics in principle examines changes over time in all forms of government, but Mill is mainly interested in the changes in democratic government, and specifically in the changes that would promote or impede the improvement of representative democracy. These changes are also the focus of the theory of development, and the change or trend that Mill most emphasizes in this theory —the trend toward equality—underlies his insistence on the importance of competence to counteract the levelling of intelligence and the growth of conformity in mass society. But this same trend also exhibits auspicious aspects. Properly nurtured and controlled, it enables more citizens to develop the capacity for appreciating higher pleasures, which include a concern for the general interest. This effect would help realize the principle of participation by improving the quality and extent of citizen activity, and would support the principle of competence by increasing the number of citizens who choose to develop their higher faculties. The theory of development thus points the way toward a gradual attenuation of the tension between the principles of participation and competence in the future, while the theory of government seeks an accommodation between the principles in the meantime.

The structure of Mill's democratic theory reflects the eclecticism that commentators have imputed to all of his thought.[1] Mill himself not only admits to adopting an eclectic approach but declares it to be a necessary and desirable feature of philosophy. Some philosophers, like Bentham, present a "one-eyed" vision of the world, singlemindedly pursuing to its logical conclusion a narrowly defined set of premises about human nature. These "half-thinkers," Mill believes, see certain aspects of the world more clearly, but their work must be supplemented by "more complete thinkers" (such as Mill) who "superadd" the insights of other philosophers.[2] In *Representative Government* Mill's aim of synthesizing the contributions of his predecessors reveals itself in the conjunction of the principles of participation and competence, either one of which alone would yield a one-eyed theory—pure democracy in the one instance, and elitism in the other. Mill's general view of the nature of political theory, as well as the overall structure of his theory of democracy, confirms that a synthesis is indeed his aim and shows that his theory (or at least his theoretical intentions) cannot be accurately characterized as either participatory or elitist in the sense in which those terms are currently used. Although the synthesis is not incoherent, it is not entirely successful either. It suffers from at least two major inadequacies: one concerns the scope of the theory; and the other, the ordering of the two basic principles in the theory.

Given Mill's aspirations for participation, especially his educative aims, we may be disappointed that the actual institutions he prescribes for achieving these goals

---

[1] See, e.g., Walter Bagehot, "The Late Mr. Mill," *The Economist* (May 7, 1873), in Norman St. John-Stevas (ed.), *The Collected Works of Walter Bagehot*, Cambridge, Mass., 1968, vol. III, pp. 555-56; and Duncan, *Marx and Mill*, pp. 209-12.

[2] Mill, "Bentham," pp. 93-94.

are so modest. The chief instruments of civic education are local government, jury duty, and free discussion. (Elsewhere he adds industrial democracy.) To be sure, these are not insignificant, and even the national political institutions he portrays go some way toward enriching participation—for example, through devices that would strengthen the relationship between representatives and their constituents. Nevertheless, the disparity between the goals of the principle of participation and the resources of Mill's participatory institutions is marked, and commentators are surely correct to criticize Mill on this count.[3] What is not correct is the implication that some of these commentators draw from the disparity. Even if the institutions of *Representative Government* offer limited scope for citizen involvement, it does not follow that an elite or the competent minority hold the real power in the political processes prescribed by Mill. The dilution of participation does not translate into dominance by the competent, for Mill's institutions also fail to give them as much political influence as the principle of competence would seem to demand.[4] Unable alone to outvote any substantial opposition even in the representative assembly, the competent minority must rely on the processes of deliberation. The competent are likely to be persuasive in these processes only insofar as civic education, in which they are expected to take the lead, has been effective. The executive is a more secure bastion for competence, but it is impotent

[3] E.g., Pateman, pp. 32-33; and Duncan, *Marx and Mill*, pp. 262-63.

[4] It is therefore misleading to suggest, as Pateman does, that Mill's commitment to participation is undercut by his permitting a "pre-determined elite . . . to gain political power" (p. 33). The problem, rather, is that neither ordinary citizens nor competent leaders may end up with sufficient power in Mill's institutions.

without the enlightened support of the legislature as well as the public. For all Mill's concern with competence, he does not in the end subject the *political* resources of the competent to serious scrutiny.

The inadequacy of Mill's institutions results partly from the conflict between his two basic principles: neither can be fully realized because each must to some degree accommodate the other. Also, the gradualism recommended by his theory of development inhibits any thoroughgoing implementation of the principles. But these constraints are not the only sources of the institutional inadequacy. The scope in which Mill's principles operate is too narrow: his theory leaves political space where neither of the principles presides at all. A great deal of power in national politics could be wielded by politicians who qualify neither as the competent minority nor as ordinary citizens. Indeed, much of contemporary democratic politics might be said to fit this pattern. Mill does not intend such a result, but he does not provide sufficient power for either the competent minority or the democratic majority to combat this "minorities rule." Theoretically, local government seems a more propitious place for encouraging participation and competence, but practically its potential for furthering these ends has been frustrated by its decline in relative power. While Mill urges that we resist this trend, he tenders no assurance that we could reverse it if we tried.

In the vast arena of organized politics outside of the government—in private associations such as trade unions, interest groups, and voluntary groups of all kinds—Mill offers little guidance for implementing the goals of participation and competence. Industrial democracy, his most promising proposal here, remains in embryonic form. It is perhaps surprising that Mill does not extend the scope of his theory to encompass non-governmental politics more than he does, having learned from Tocqueville that participatory practices in the society at large are indispensable for a healthy democracy. However, a chief obstacle to realizing participation in this wider context has become the bureaucratic and oligarchic character of private associations. Mill is handicapped in seeing this problem because he regards bureaucracy mainly as a form of government, instead of as a form of organization inherent in many kinds of social and political activity. Since the problem of satisfying the principles of participation and competence in a bureaucratic government resembles in some measure the problem of satisfying them in private associations, Mill perhaps could have extrapolated his conclusions about bureaucracy to the government of interest groups and other private associations. But he did not do so.

A theory that conjoins two principles that are sometimes in conflict needs to encompass a greater range of social and political activity than do single-principle theories. Within any limited sphere of activity a theory cannot fully realize two conflicting principles because compromises have to be made between them, but if the theory is applied to a wider range of phenomena, the losses resulting from the compromises in any one sphere of activity can often be compensated by gains in other spheres. Also, since even within the area of governmental activity Mill by default leaves much uncontrolled by either principle, his theory would have to be extended to provide greater opportunities for citizen participation and competent leadership, especially in national politics.

Even if the scope of Mill's theory can be widened in these ways, a further problem remains: the theoretical indeterminacy of the balance between the principles of participation and competence. It is perfectly sensible for Mill to leave the precise balance between the principles to be worked out in practice within the guidelines proposed by the theory of government and the theory of development. No democratic theorist should be expected to anticipate all the variations in social and political circumstances in which his theory may apply. Mill's theory, however, is indeterminate in a more debilitating sense. It provides no satisfactory way to choose between courses of action that would further participation and those that would improve competence, when these values conflict. A natural way of dealing with such conflicts would be to seek an optimal balance in which the total combined value of the two principles is maximized. To do this, however, we must be able to compare, in a reasonably precise manner, a loss in one value with a gain in the other, and it is difficult to see how we could ever *justify* a function that would relate values as different as participation and competence. Faced with this difficulty, Mill would call on the concept of utility to serve as a common measure of the two values. The principles of participation and competence, like many other moral and political precepts, could be treated as what Mill describes as "secondary principles," which often contradict each other and leave us in doubt about what to do. In "cases of conflict between secondary principles it is requisite that first principles be appealed to," and the ultimate first principle—utility—is the "common umpire" to decide which secondary principle should take precedence.[5] Mill sees this capacity to escape from indeterminacy as the great merit of utilitarianism compared to other ethical theories, and indeed in pure

[5] *Utilitarianism*, ch. II, 224-26, ch. V, 251-55. Cf. *Logic*, Bk. VI, ch. xii, § 7, pp. 951-52.

forms of utilitarianism like Bentham's it is a significant advantage (whatever disadvantages such theories may have). But Mill has forfeited the advantage by adding a qualitative dimension to the concept of utility. The doctrine of higher pleasures, on which the principle of competence rests, postulates qualitative values that by their nature are not commensurate with quantitative ones, nor even with each other. A conflict between participation and competence thus would remain unresolved by the principle of utility; the conflict is built into the concept of utility as Mill presents it.

Were we to grant that the values expressed by Mill's two principles could be compared so that an optimal balance could be determined, we would still be without a way to decide which principle should take precedence in some instances of conflict between them. Suppose that we face a choice between a reform that would attain a higher optimum level by realizing greater participation and another reform that would achieve an equally high optimum by realizing greater competence. On Mill's theory there would be no way to choose between these two reforms. More importantly, his theory would permit a substantial loss in participation (even below present levels) in return for a large gain in competence if the net gain resulted in a higher optimum level. That is, we might be forced to choose (a) changes that would improve the competence of leadership while reducing the level of participation, rather than (b) changes that would yield a lesser improvement in competence of leadership while maintaining or even increasing participation. Because participation is supposed to generate greater competence, Mill hopes that occasions for such hard choices will not be common. But when these choices become necessary, Mill's theory proffers little or no assistance. That his theory is indeterminate in this way is not a fatal objection if it can be amended as I suggest below. Nor is this objection a reason for preferring contemporary democratic theories, since those that come closest to acknowledging a range of values as extensive as Mill's suffer from the same indeterminacy.

MILL AND SOCIAL SCIENCE

Mill's theory of democracy cannot be neatly divided into empirical and normative parts. Even though some of the key propositions Mill puts forward can be regarded as mainly normative or mainly empirical, the theories of government and development, as well as all of his major arguments, employ not only both kinds of propositions but also various hybrids of them. In this respect Mill follows the example of the leading political theorists of the past and departs from the practice of twentieth-century social scientists and theorists who turn a logically acceptable distinction between normative and empirical statements into a dichotomy between kinds of theories. Since it would therefore distort Mill's theory to segregate its empirical and normative aspects, this study has sought to prevent these categories from shaping the presentation of the structure of that theory. However, to compare the theory with the work of social scientists who take these categories more seriously, we have to isolate its empirical aspects. Doing so will not cause any serious harm so long as we keep in mind the larger context of Mill's general theory in which these empirical propositions and approaches are situated.

The empirical aspects of Mill's theory relate to recent social science in two general ways. First, many of Mill's specific propositions are supported by, or (more usually) are consistent with, its findings. For example, some evidence upholds his claims that participation makes government more responsive to citizens, and that participation is associated with higher levels of economic prosperity and various forms of civic education. The support is limited because in these studies the conditions in which the participation takes place are not equivalent to the ideal conditions Mill postulates, and because the studies do not establish the causal direction of the processes. The results of other studies are compromised because their basic concepts are inadequately specified: the United States is probably more conformist than other democracies to which Mill compared it, but exactly what conformity means and how it is related to consensus remains unclear. Some of the predictions Mill makes are approximately correct but are either premature or insufficiently qualified. The belief that the kind of deference favored by Bagehot would decline is an example of the former, and the assertion that the trend toward equality would continue is an illustration of the latter. Still others seem to accord with evidence we now have, but many social scientists would disagree with the interpretations Mill would give of the evidence. Here examples include Mill's observations on the advantages of the Hare system, the decline of the legislative role of representative assemblies, and certain features of what has been called post-industrial society.

Some of Mill's empirical propositions have turned out to be simply false. For example, modern economies did not become stationary (at least not in the way Mill expected), and class conflict, while growing less patent, did not disappear. If only the predictions were at issue, we might be prepared to say again that they are merely premature and that they might be vindicated sometime in the future. But the economic and sociological analysis underlying the predictions is faulty, a failing that would vitiate Mill's general theory even if his particular predictions turned out to be correct. Nevertheless, like some other flaws in Mill's empirical inquiry, this one could be corrected without altering the basic structure of his democratic theory. To account for economic growth, Mill would have to abandon some essential elements in his economic analysis, but he could fit such an account into his theory of development quite naturally, perhaps even more naturally than the assumption of a stationary state, which runs contrary to most of the other trends posited by that theory. He would then be better able to explain the diminution of overt class conflict, which on his original theory should not have occurred until greater redistribution had taken place. More generally, we should remember that Mill, after all, expected his theories to be revised in light of future experience, and that he gave good methodological reasons for doubting the reliability of long-range predictions made in his time (or at any other time).

The second way in which Mill's theory relates to recent social science is more indirect and elusive. It involves, not specific propositions, but his general approach —the selection of problems, overall interpretations of certain developments, and the emphases of explanations. Mill's theory remains pertinent, first, because his approach to some problems parallels recent work and, second (and more importantly), because his approach to other problems challenges recent orthodoxy. An example of the first is Mill's critique of the idea of a rational bureaucracy, which, though limited to a form of government, raises issues otherwise similar to those discussed by modern critics of Weber. Also, the conception of the role of the representative set forth in *Representative Government* coincides with the most satisfactory modern analyses of that role. On the matter of local government, many contemporary observers agree with Mill that different local issues require different sizes of governmental units, that the exact balance between centralization and decentralization must be worked out in practice, and that local government (properly constituted) should be strengthened. Mill's account of political stability, incomplete though it is, emphasizes attitudes and beliefs as explanatory factors, just as some modern analyses do. These anticipations show that Mill's theory is not remote from the concerns of current social science and, in that sense, is not obsolete as some commentators have claimed.

Nothing in these parallels of course justifies Mill's treatment of the problems he considers, not only because the approaches remain controversial among social scientists but more significantly because even a widely accepted approach may be misconceived. Part of the value of a theory such as Mill's inheres in the critical perspective it furnishes. If Mill's approach were identical to prevailing views in social science, we would have much less reason to take Mill's theory seriously. But, as we have noticed, Mill's theory challenges conventional social science in various ways. Mill does not, for example, accept the necessity of strong party government for effective, stable democracy, and he points to some of the dangers it occasions. The significance of his critical perspective is further underscored when its application to recent democratic theories is considered in the next section.

Two sets of problems with Mill's theory cannot be overcome simply by correcting his substantive propositions or by treating his approach as a critical challenge, for the problems arise from defects in his methodology. First of all, Mill's ambivalence about the use of the comparative method leaves his efforts toward empirical verification in a kind of methodological limbo. The *Logic* sets very strict standards for confirming the hypotheses of comparative analysis. To establish the effects of a certain causal factor in one society, we must, Mill insists, compare that society with another that is the same in every respect except for the absence of the factor in question. Since, as Mill acknowledges, such similarities are at best rare, rigorous comparative analysis would hardly ever be possible. Evidently Mill accepts this conclusion in *Representative Government* because he makes few genuine comparisons there between political systems. Most of those he does make are merely casual illustrations either of unwise departures from the practices he recommends or of acceptable variations justified by different social conditions. The direct election of judges in the United States is an example of the first; the indirect election of Senators, of the second.[6] Yet (although the British model of parliamentary democracy always lingers at least in the background) Mill presents his theory in a general form, framed to apply to any society that satisfies the minimal conditions for maintaining representative government at all. He seems to assume that the differences between societies that have achieved this level of development are relatively insignificant for his theory.

But in fact Mill cannot escape the need to conduct comparative analysis. His theory of government not only allows for, but often requires, variations in the institutions he prescribes, depending on the different social

[6] *CRG*, ch. IX, p. 194; ch. XIV, p. 265.

contexts in which they exist. Mill usually admits as much. But he does not venture to show how his institutional recommendations might be modified for these different contexts, even where the context very much affects whether or not the institutions will do what he intends them to do. For example, in a highly segmented society, the system of Personal Representation might not result in the selection of any "national" representatives at all because each class would be likely to choose candidates to represent its own interests exclusively. Perhaps we should not expect Mill to spell out all of the variations that institutions could take in different kinds of societies, but we are entitled to know about some of the major modifications that would be necessary to realize the basic principles of his theory, at least where the principles rely so significantly on social conditions that vary markedly in different societies.

Another reason that Mill cannot do without comparative analysis is that many of his crucial arguments explicitly rest on empirical comparisons—for example, that participation makes a difference in governmental responsiveness, or that an active national character promotes social progress. Others, such as the educative argument for participation, cry out for comparative evidence that Mill does not supply. *Representative Government* does not follow up the promising start at comparative analysis Mill earlier made while arguing against Tocqueville's conclusion that equality of conditions alone accounts for conformity. There Mill began to isolate factors in a systematic way, and the analysis, though falling short of the standard set in the *Logic*, nevertheless grappled with some of the questions implied by that standard. In *Representative Government* it is almost as if Mill has decided that the standard is so impossible to meet that he will not attempt even to approximate it. Yet he offers nothing in its place. The inverse-deductive method, acceptable enough as a general approach to empirical inquiry, furnishes no specific guidance for verifying comparisons. Neither can the theory of development substitute for a comparative method, since that theory has a different purpose and in any case has problems of its own. If, as Mill hoped, sociology ultimately could be based on psychology, general political theories such as his theory of democracy could more readily dispense with comparative analysis, since presumably they would rest on psychological propositions that are supposed to be universal.[7] But the science of ethology, which is to be the connecting link in this reductionist program, remains only in outline in the *Logic* and is very little in evidence in *Representative Government*, forcing Mill to rely on an assortment of unsystematic assumptions about human nature. The *Logic* thus leaves Mill without the comparative method he urgently needs in *Representative Government* and also encourages him to believe that he can do without one.

The second set of methodological problems concerns the theory of development, which, Mill freely concedes, is not a finished product. However, it has problems that do not stem from its incompleteness. Of those already mentioned, the most significant one arises from Mill's attempt to account for development by a single factor, the "speculative faculties of mankind." Since Mill believes that a single-factor approach is possible and that he has found that factor, he does not explore what seems a sensible alternative—the possibility of formulating a

[7] On Mill's reductionist program, see Ryan, *Mill*, 1970, pp. 156-62.

reasonably systematic theory that allows for multiple causes, irreducible to a single prime cause. Mill anyhow would be reluctant to admit a plurality of basic causes. Without a single prime cause we would not be able to identify a "central chain" that would order all of the other factors or causes in the process of development; the consequence, he apparently supposes, would be a very disorderly theory.[8] Moreover, abandoning the particular prime cause Mill favors would have far-reaching implications not only for his theory of development but also for his theory of democracy. The assumption that ideas, through the process of rational deliberation in social and political life, are the primary agent for furthering civic education and political competence pervades the entire fabric of his democratic theory. It would of course be possible to attribute some political efficacy to ideas even on a multi-factor theory of development, but a great deal more analysis, more complex than any Mill offers, would be necessary to execute such an approach and render it consistent with the aims of his democratic theory.

The theory of development is the weakest element in Mill's theory of democracy, but most of its weaknesses stem from its ambitious aims. He dares to take on the larger questions that many social scientists now put aside, perhaps because like natural scientists they wish to "study the most important problems they think they can solve," considering it "their professional business to solve problems, not merely grapple with them."[9] But Mill could not endorse so circumscribed a conception of

[8] *Logic*, Bk. vi, ch. x, § 7, p. 925.
[9] P. B. Medawar, *The Art of the Soluble*, London, 1967, pp. 7, 85-87.

theory, however modest an agenda for current research he might be prepared to accept. He thought it important not only to discover the chief cause of political development but also to identify, and to find ways to encourage, long-term trends in the process of the improvement of democracy. If some of these concerns are not entirely absent in the social science of this century, they are rarely united in a systematic theory. Contemporary social science can learn a great deal not only from Mill's mistakes but also from his ambitions.

MILL AND MODERN DEMOCRATIC THEORY

During the past several decades elitist democratic theory has been the dominant view in academic literature on democracy, and the single most influential theorist of this orientation has probably been Joseph Schumpeter. His theory designates the competition of leaders for political office as the defining attribute of democracy and limits the role of citizens to choosing among those leaders in periodic elections.[10] Some modern theorists following Schumpeter encourage somewhat more participation, while others reaffirm with even more fervor his opposition to greater participation. But all still regard the nature of the elite or leadership echelon as the crucial concern for democratic theory.[11] At the same time some

[10] Schumpeter, pp. 269, 272.

[11] The theorists most commonly discussed in this group include (besides Schumpeter): Bernard R. Berelson et al., *Voting*, Chicago, 1954, esp. pp. 305-23; Dahl, *Preface* and *Who Governs?*; John Plamenatz, "Electoral Studies and Democratic Theory: A British View," *Political Studies* 6 (Feb. 1958), pp. 1-9; Lipset, *Political Man*, pp. 403-17; Key, *Public Opinion*, esp. pp. 535-38; and Giovanni Sartori, *Democratic Theory*, New York, 1965. For other references, see Bachrach, *passim*.

of these writers—the pluralists among them—extend their theories to embrace group politics.[12] Where Schumpeter permitted no "political backseat driving" between elections, the pluralists see parties and pressure groups as vehicles for influencing government more or less continually. They believe that these groups, though enlisting relatively few citizens, force leaders to pay attention to all important interests in society, and that this "minorities rule" yields policies that come as close as possible to expressing the general interest.

More recently critics have mounted an assault against elitist theorists of democracy and their pluralist companions.[13] The critics charge that elitist theorists ignore the educative aims of participation, concentrating only on the protective function of participation, and that they generally take a static view of democracy, emphasizing

[12] The pluralist writers most often mentioned include: Arthur F. Bentley, *The Process of Government*, Bloomington, Ind., 1949; David Truman, *The Governmental Process*, New York, 1951; Nelson W. Polsby, *Community Power and Political Theory*, New Haven, 1963; and Dahl's earlier writings cited above. For a good summary and critique, see Geraint Parry, *Political Elites*, New York, 1969, pp. 64-94.

[13] The critics include: Duncan and Lukes, pp. 156-77; Lane Davis, "The Cost of Realism," *Western Political Quarterly* 17 (March 1964), pp. 37-46; Bottomore, *Elites*, pp. 105-21; Bay, pp. 39-51; Walker, pp. 286-95; Charles Taylor, "Neutrality in Political Science," in Peter Laslett and W. G. Runciman (eds.), *Philosophy, Politics and Society*, 3d series, New York, 1967, pp. 25-57; Bachrach, pp. 10-64; J. Peter Euben, "Political Science and Political Silence," in Philip Green and Sanford Levinson (eds.), *Power and Community*, New York, 1969, pp. 3-58; and Pateman, pp. 1-21. Quentin Skinner attacks both the critics and the theorists they are criticizing in "The Empirical Theorists of Democracy and Their Critics," *Political Theory* 1 (Aug. 1973), pp. 287-306. Plamenatz has himself sharply attacked the elitists (or revisionists) but without changing his own theory in a way that would remove him from the revisionist category as defined by most other critics (*Democracy and Illusion*, London, 1973).

stability rather than improvement. For both of these reasons elitist theorists fail to recognize that increases in opportunities for participation may be possible and desirable. Mill's argument for civic education and his theory of development provide bases for recognizing this. Consequently, *Representative Government,* unlike some of his earlier writings, assigns a greater role to citizens than do Schumpeter and most other elitist theorists of democracy. Citizens, for example, should consider issues when they choose representatives and should to some extent control their representatives even between elections. Mill's theory also suggests a reply to the argument from apathy used by some elitist theorists and casts doubt on the pluralists' confidence in the outcome of group politics.

Even if the critics elaborate some of these complaints about elitist democratic theory more fully than Mill does, none presents them as a part of a full-scale theory of democracy, as Mill does, so that their relationships to each other and to other aspects of democratic theory can be appreciated. Even if the theory of development, for instance, does not succeed, Mill shows that some such doctrine is necessary for a complete theory of democracy, and that a static perspective on democracy is insufficient. It is no accident that most of the twentieth-century democratic theorists who favor participation much in the spirit of Mill also seem to be searching for a theory of development akin to Mill's, whereas most elitist theorists of democracy appear to reject such a theory out of hand, if they consider one at all.[14] Yet the critics who complain about the elitists' neglect of improvement do not, as Mill does, venture to construct a theoretical foundation for their objections. Some apparently do not

[14] See Thompson, pp. 19-22 and 23-24.

even see a need for such a theory as part of the case for greater participation.

Mill adds still another important dimension that is missing in the contemporary critiques of elitist democratic theory. While much of the critics' case against that theory is convincing, they do not come to grips with one of the chief reasons that provoked the elitists to revise "classical" democratic theory in the first place— the necessity and desirability of competent leadership. Some of the critics give the impression that they envision a society of leaderless citizens, each fulfilling his or her potential for self-government, untrammeled by the presence of any superior authority. Rushing to restore the principle of participation to its rightful position in democratic theory, the critics fail to reserve a proper place for the principle of competence. It is revealing that in their explanations of the rise of elitist theory, few critics concede that such theory might have been animated partly by a recognition of the need for leadership. Generally, the critics mention instead ideological and historical factors, such as the fears of instability and totalitarianism.[15]

Mill's theory has the great virtue of preserving the commitment to participation that the critics urge while recognizing the importance of competence that the elitist theorists of democracy stress. This promising marriage is not of course completely consummated in Mill's theory

[15] E.g., Duncan and Lukes, pp. 174-77; Davis, p. 44; Bay, p. 41; Euben, pp. 3-17; and Pateman, pp. 2-3. Bachrach (pp. 1-9) and Bottomore (*Elites*, p. 104) are exceptions to this generalization. One of the few contemporary theorists who attends to the requirements of leadership in democratic theory but without sacrificing the demands of participation is J. Roland Pennock, "Democracy and Leadership," in William N. Chambers and Robert H. Salisbury (eds.), *Democracy Today*, New York, 1962, pp. 122-58.

because the balance between participation and competence is theoretically indeterminate. But the same may be said of the most recent theory that, like Mill's, attempts to unite the values of participation and competence in a single conceptual structure. Robert Dahl's criterion of personal choice (that political decisions conform to citizens' preferences) captures part of the content of the participation principle, while his criterion of competence (that decisions be made by the most qualified persons) and the criterion of economy (that the political process minimize the amount of time and energy citizens expend) roughly correspond to Mill's principle of competence.[16] Dahl seeks an "optimum mix" or "balance" of these criteria, trading off one against the other to achieve the highest combined value of the three, instead of maximizing any one.[17] Thus, unlike elitist theorists, Dahl does not allow the requisites of leadership consistently to dominate the demand for greater participation. However, Dahl's optimum mix is indeterminate in much the same way that Mill's is, and in this respect Dahl's theory also founders on the difficulty of devising a formula for comparing marginal changes in the values to which his criteria refer. Further, Dahl's theory is deficient in another way in which Mill's is not: Dahl's criterion of personal choice omits the educative value of participation.[18] This value could not be easily

[16] Dahl, *After the Revolution?* New Haven, 1970, pp. 8-56. This work gives considerably more emphasis to participation than Dahl's earlier writings and should not be regarded as an example of an elitist democratic theory, however his earlier writings may be characterized.

[17] Dahl, *Revolution*, pp. 39, 48-49, 52, 56, 79.

[18] Cf. *Revolution*, pp. 8-28. In *Polyarchy* the key characteristic of democracy he chooses to mention is "the continuing responsiveness of the government to the preferences of citizens. . ." (p. 1).

appended to his theory, either, since part of the point of including this value in a theory is to stress that citizens can discover new preferences and change old ones. This point is hard to articulate in a theory that, like Dahl's, is cast in a language implying that the preferences of citizens already exist, ready to be expressed when the opportunity arises.

If Mill in this way offers a more comprehensive foundation for democratic theory, he still lacks a method for resolving conflicts between his two basic principles without recourse either to a formula that would compare marginal changes in the values expressed by each principle or to a common measure into which the values could be translated. An attractive alternative—though perhaps not one that Mill himself would have endorsed —is a rule that assigns priority to one of the two basic principles. With such a rule we could more easily decide between changes that favor competence and those that favor participation, at least where both are realized to some minimal degree. Despite important differences between Mill's theory and modern contract theory as developed by John Rawls, the notion of "lexical priority" in Rawls' theory is a promising place to look for a priority rule that would help order the two basic principles in Mill's theory. Rawls uses this notion to rank his first principle of justice (which protects equal basic liberties) ahead of his second principle of justice (which deals with social and economic inequalities).[19] The priority rule holds that liberty "can be restricted only for the sake of liberty itself." To justify any restrictions on the right of equal participation (one kind of basic liberty), we must show that "from the perspective of the repre-

[19] Rawls, pp. 243-51, 541-48. The complete statement of the two principles of justice and the priority rules is at pp. 302-3.

sentative citizen in the constitutional convention the less extensive freedom of participation is sufficiently outweighed by the greater security and extent of the other liberties."[20] We cannot appeal to any compensatory economic and social benefits, including improvements in the competence of leaders to achieve these benefits.

However, Rawls' formulation of the priority rule does not really help decide between the principles of participation and competence. One could maintain (and elitist democratic theorists in effect so argue) that promoting the principle of competence alone actually supports "greater security and extent of the other liberties." The rule, moreover, does not recognize participation in the full sense that Mill (usually) stresses and that the critics of elitist democratic theory affirm. As Rawls himself points out, Mill's argument for plural voting (which is inconsistent with aspects of his case for participation) can be perfectly compatible with the priority rule.[21] Furthermore, Rawls' criteria for participation (equal political liberty) are approximately the same as Dahl's and, hence, are similarly defective.[22] Although Rawls later mentions values that correspond to the educative goal of participation, his priority rule evidently does not require that this goal be furthered in order to justify restrictions on participation.[23]

Nevertheless, we can formulate a priority rule, formally similar to Rawls', that would stipulate that the principle of participation take precedence over the principle of competence: greater competence in leadership

[20] Rawls, pp. 244, 229. Lexical priority operates only after a society has reached a certain minimum level of material well-being.

[21] Rawls, pp. 232-33.

[22] Rawls, pp. 224-25. Rawls, in fact, endorses Dahl's criteria.

[23] Rawls, pp. 233-34.

is acceptable to the extent that it also tends to increase opportunities for participation. On this formulation, to justify a departure from the principle of participation to implement the principle of competence more fully, we would have to show that the increase in competence itself tends to improve participation at least in the future. Such a rule could also serve as a basis for assessing the nature of democratic leadership. We could examine some of the same phenomena on which elitist theorists focus—for example, the recruitment and social background of leaders, their beliefs and attitudes, and the nature of competition among leaders—but with more attention to the impact of these phenomena on participation. A pattern of leadership that encourages significantly greater participation by citizens would, on this view, be better than one that offers fewer opportunities, even if the former attained a lower level of competence than the latter, provided that some minimum level of competence (which would have to be specified) were maintained.[24]

It is not obvious that Mill, faced with deciding which of his basic principles should have priority, would have

[24] A strict criterion of lexical priority would entail choosing an infinitesimal increase in participation over a very large gain in competence, but in practice a lexical criterion could allow for some crude relative weighting of participation and competence within a specified range. For this purpose a rough approximation of what is to count as "significantly greater participation" would need to be indicated. Since this approximation would not have to be so precise as the values employed in a trade-off criterion, the use of even the less strict lexical criterion would differ from that of trade-off criteria. For criticism of the idea of lexical priority, however, see Brian Barry and Douglas W. Rae, "Political Evaluation," in Fred Greenstein and Nelson W. Polsby (eds.), *Political Science: Scope and Theory*, Reading, Mass., 1975, pp. 351-53, and Barry, *Liberal Theory*, pp. 59-82.

actually chosen the principle of participation, since in *Representative Government* he tenaciously straddles the fence between participation and competence. But still within the general perspective of his theory we could construct an argument for the priority of the principle of participation, based on the claim that it is more comprehensive than the principle of competence. If the principle of participation were fully realized, the values expressed by the principle of competence would also be fulfilled—given Mill's assumption that citizens become more competent as they take a more active role in politics. In contrast, if the principle of competence were fully realized, the values expressed by the principle of participation would not necessarily be fulfilled—no matter how valid any of Mill's assumptions may be. The reason for this asymmetry between the principles, when they are extrapolated to their ideal limits, is that the principle of competence by its nature does not attribute any independent value to having citizens make political decisions themselves. By their example competent leaders could further the civic education of citizens, but by this process alone citizens would not fully enjoy the educative fruits of participation nor could they secure its protective benefits. Therefore, even ideally the principle of competence would not fulfill the educative aim of participation, while the principle of participation ideally would satisfy the goals of the principle of competence. This argument still depends on the assumption that participation and competence can eventually be reconciled. We can purge Mill's theory of its indeterminacy, but not of its pervasive hope that the important values in democracy ultimately cohere. Mill's theory exposes many of the conflicts between these values and does so in a more systematic and consistent manner than many of his critics recognize and than many modern theories do. But in his eagerness to reconcile all the good things in political life he leaves much undone.

Despite its deficiencies, Mill's theory of democracy remains superior in many respects to much contemporary theorizing about democracy. It can still serve as a guide for identifying omissions in modern theories and as a foundation for developing democratic theory in the future. Mill not only anticipates many of the recent criticisms of contemporary democratic theory but, more importantly, creates a theoretical structure that comprehends those criticisms as well as crucial values that the critics themselves overlook. Those who contemplate the present and future condition of representative democracy would therefore be unwise to disregard the teachings of *Representative Government*.

Bibliography

Only works cited in the footnotes are included here. For more extensive bibliographies, see the *Bibliography of the Published Writings of John Stuart Mill*, ed. Ney MacMinn, J. R. Hainds, and James M. McCrimmon (Evanston, Ill.: Northwestern University Press, 1945); and *The Mill News Letter* (Toronto: Toronto University Press, 1965—).

The Collected Works of John Stuart Mill, edited by John M. Robson and published by Toronto University Press, is used for all the writings that have been so far published in this excellent edition; references to this edition are abbreviated as *CW*. I have used the third library edition of *Considerations on Representative Government* (London: Longman, Green, Longman, Roberts and Green, 1865), which incorporates some material not in the earlier editions; and the first library edition of *On Liberty* (London: John W. Parker and Son, 1859), which differs in a few significant respects from the more widely available versions based on the People's Edition. The best edition of the *Autobiography* is the one edited by Jack Stillinger (Boston: Houghton Mifflin, 1969). *DD* refers to the five-volume edition of *Dissertations and Discussions* (New York: Henry Holt and Company, 1873-1875).

Dates in brackets at the end of entries for Mill's works indicate the year of original publication.

WORKS OF MILL

Auguste Comte and Positivism, in *CW,* Toronto, 1969, vol. x, pp. 260-368. [1865]

Autobiography and Other Writings, ed. Jack Stillinger, Boston, 1969. [1873]

"Bentham," in *CW,* Toronto, 1969, vol. x, pp. 75-115. [1838]

"Centralisation," *Edinburgh Review* 115 (April 1862), pp. 323-358.

"Chapters on Socialism," in *CW,* Toronto, 1967, vol. v, pp. 703-753. [1879]

"Civilization," in *DD,* New York, 1874, vol. I, pp. 186-231. [1836]

"Coleridge," in *CW,* Toronto, 1969, vol. x, pp. 117-163. [1840]

Considerations on Representative Government, 3d ed., London, 1865. [1861]

The Earlier Letters of John Stuart Mill, 1812-1848, ed. Francis E. Mineka, in *CW,* Toronto, 1963, vols. XII-XIII.

"A Few Observations on the French Revolution," in *DD,* New York, 1874, vol. I, pp. 82-88. [1833]

"Grote's Aristotle," in *DD,* New York, 1875, vol. v, pp. 169-215. [1873]

"Grote's Plato," in *DD,* New York, 1874, vol. IV, pp. 227-331. [1866]

"Guizot's Essays and Lectures on History," in *DD,* New York, 1874, vol. II, pp. 297-362. [1845]

Inaugural Address at St. Andrews, in *DD,* New York, 1874, vol. IV, pp. 332-407. [1867]

The Later Letters of John Stuart Mill, 1849-1873, ed. Francis E. Mineka and Dwight N. Lindley, in *CW,* Toronto, 1972, vols. XIV-XVII.

"Michelet's History of France," in *DD*, New York, 1874, vol. II, pp. 198-259. [1844]

"Notes on the Newspapers," *Monthly Repository* 8 (April 1834), pp. 309-312.

"On Genius," *Monthly Repository* 6 (October 1832), pp. 649-659.

On Liberty, London, 1854.

"Papers Relating to the Re-organization of the Civil Service," *Parliamentary Papers*, 1854-1855, vol. XX, pp. 92-98.

"Parliamentary Proceedings of the Session," *London Review* 1 (July 1835), pp. 512-524 [vol. 30 of *Westminster Review*].

Personal Representation: Speech of John Stuart Mill, Esq., M.P. Delivered in the House of Commons, May 29, 1867, London, 1867.

Principles of Political Economy, in *CW*, Toronto, 1965, vols. II-III. [1848, 1871]

"The Rationale of Political Representation," *London Review* 1 (July 1835), pp. 341-371 [vol. 30 of *Westminster Review*].

"Recent Writers on Reform," in *DD*, New York, 1874, vol. IV, pp. 51-100. [1859]

"Remarks on Bentham's Philosophy," in *CW*, vol. X, pp. 3-18. [1833]

"The Spirit of the Age," in *The Examiner* (January 23, 1831), pp. 50-52 [complete work in F.A. Hayek (ed.), *The Spirit of the Age*, Chicago, 1942].

The Subjection of Women, London, 1869.

A System of Logic: Ratiocinative and Inductive, in *CW*, Toronto, 1973, 1974, vols. VII-VIII. [1843, 1872]

Thoughts on Parliamentary Reform, in *DD*, New York, 1874, vol. IV, pp. 5-50. [1859]

Three Essays on Religion, in *CW*, vol. x, pp. 369-489.
[1874]
"M. de Tocqueville on Democracy in America," in *DD*,
New York, 1874, vol. II, pp. 79-161. [1840]
"De Tocqueville on Democracy in America," *London
Review* 2 (October 1835), pp. 85-129 [vol. 31 of *West-
minster Review*].
Utilitarianism, in *CW*, vol. x, pp. 203-259. [1861]
"Vindication of the French Revolution of February,
1848, in Reply to Lord Brougham and Others," in
DD, New York, 1873, vol. III, pp. 5-92. [1849]

WORKS ABOUT MILL

Annan, Noel. "John Stuart Mill," in Hugh S. Davies
and George Watson (eds.), *The English Mind: Stud-
ies in the English Moralists Presented to Basil Willey*,
Cambridge, England, 1964, pp. 219-239.
Anschutz, R. P. *The Philosophy of J. S. Mill*, Oxford,
1963.
Bagehot, Walter. "The Late Mr. Mill," *The Economist*
(May 7, 1873), in Norman St. John-Stevas (ed.), *The
Collected Works of Walter Bagehot*, Cambridge,
Mass., 1968, vol. III, pp. 555-556.
Burns, J. H. "J. S. Mill and Democracy, 1829-61," *Po-
litical Studies* 5 (June 1957), pp. 158-175, 5 (October
1957), pp. 281-294.
Cowling, Maurice. *Mill and Liberalism*, Cambridge,
England, 1963.
Cumming, Robert. *Human Nature and History: A
Study of Liberal Political Thought*, 2 vols., Chicago,
1969.
Duncan, Graeme. "John Stuart Mill and Democracy,"
Politics 4 (May 1969), pp. 67-83.

————. *Marx and Mill: Two Views of Social Conflict and Social Harmony*, Cambridge, England, 1973.

Gorovitz, Samuel (ed.). *Mill: Utilitarianism*, Indianapolis, 1971.

Halliday, R. J. "Some Recent Interpretations of John Stuart Mill," *Philosophy* 43 (January 1968), pp. 1-17.

Hamburger, Joseph. *Intellectuals in Politics: John Stuart Mill and the Philosophic Radicals*, New Haven, 1965.

Harris, Abram L. "John Stuart Mill's Theory of Progress," *Ethics* 66 (April 1956), pp. 157-174.

Himmelfarb, Gertrude. *On Liberty and Liberalism: The Case of John Stuart Mill*, New York, 1974.

Holthoon, F. L. van. *The Road to Utopia: A Study of John Stuart Mill's Social Thought*, Assen, The Netherlands, 1971.

Kendall, Willmoore, and George W. Carey. "The 'Roster Device': J. S. Mill and Contemporary Elitism," *Western Political Quarterly* 21 (March 1968), pp. 20-39.

Kern, Paul B. "Universal Suffrage Without Democracy: Thomas Hare and J. S. Mill," *Review of Politics* 34 (July 1972), pp. 306-322.

Letwin, Shirley. *The Pursuit of Certainty: David Hume, Jeremy Bentham, John Stuart Mill, Beatrice Webb*. Cambridge, England, 1965.

Lindsay, A. D. "Introduction," in *Utilitarianism, Liberty and Representative Government*, New York, 1951.

Mandelbaum, Maurice. "On Interpreting Mill's Utilitarianism," *Journal of the History of Philosophy* 6 (January 1968), pp. 35-46.

Mayer, David Y. "John Stuart Mill and Classical Democracy," *Politics* 3 (May 1968), pp. 55-64.

Mazlish, Bruce. *James and John Stuart Mill: Father and Son in the Nineteenth Century*, New York, 1975.

McCloskey, H. J. *John Stuart Mill: A Critical Study*, London, 1971.

McNiece, Gerald. "Shelley, John Stuart Mill and the Secret Ballot," *Mill News Letter* 8 (Spring 1973), pp. 2-7.

Millet, René. "Le Parti Radical en Angleterre: un manifeste de M. Stuart Mill," *Revue des Deux Mondes* 97 (February 15, 1872), pp. 932-959.

Packe, Michael St. John. *The Life of John Stuart Mill*, London, 1954.

Plamenatz, John. *The English Utilitarians*, 2d ed., Oxford, 1958.

Radcliff, Peter (ed.). *Limits of Liberty: Studies of Mill's On Liberty*, Belmont, Calif., 1966.

Robson, John M. *The Improvement of Mankind: The Social and Political Thought of John Stuart Mill*, Toronto, 1968.

Ryan, Alan. *J. S. Mill*, London, 1974.

———. *John Stuart Mill*, New York, 1970.

———. "Two Concepts of Politics and Democracy: James and John Stuart Mill," in Martin Fleisher (ed.), *Machiavelli and the Nature of Political Thought*, New York, 1972, pp. 76-113.

———. "Utilitarianism and Bureaucracy: The Views of J. S. Mill," in Gillian Sutherland (ed.), *Studies in the Growth of Nineteenth-Century Government*, London, 1972, pp. 33-62.

Schwartz, Pedro. *The New Political Economy of J. S. Mill*, Durham, N.C., 1972.

Stephen, James Fitzjames. *Liberty, Equality, Fraternity*, Cambridge, England, 1967.

Stephen, Leslie. *The English Utilitarians*, London, 1900.

———. "Social Macadamisation," *Fraser's Magazine*, n.s. 6 (August 1872), pp. 150-168.

OTHER WORKS CITED

Adams, John Clarke. *The Quest for Democratic Law: The Role of Parliament in the Legislative Process*, New York, 1970.

Adelman, Irma, and Cynthia Taft Morris. *Society, Politics, and Economic Development*, Baltimore, 1967.

Agger, Robert E., Daniel Goldrich, and Bert E. Swanson. *The Rulers and the Ruled: Political Power and Impotence in American Communities*, New York, 1964.

Albrow, Martin. *Bureaucracy*, New York, 1970.

Alford, Robert. *Party and Society: The Anglo-American Democracies*, Chicago, 1963.

Almond, Gabriel, and Sidney Verba. *The Civic Culture: Political Attitudes and Democracy in Five Nations*, Princeton, 1963.

Anderson, Charles H. *The Political Economy of Social Class*, Englewood Cliffs, N.J., 1974.

Andreano, Ralph (ed.). *New Views on American Economic Development*, Cambridge, Mass., 1965.

Aristotle. *Politics*, tr. H. Rackham, Cambridge, Mass., 1967.

———. *The Politics of Aristotle*, tr. and ed. Ernest Barker, Oxford, 1962.

Aron, Raymond. *The Opium of the Intellectuals*, tr. Terence Kilmartin, London, 1957.

———. *Progress and Disillusion: The Dialectics of Modern Society*, New York, 1968.

Asch, Solomon E. "Effects of Group Pressure upon the Modification and Distortion of Judgment," in H. Guetzkow (ed.), *Groups, Leadership and Men*, Pittsburgh, 1951, pp. 177-190.

Atkinson, John W., and Norman T. Feather (eds.). *A Theory of Achievement Motivation*, New York, 1966.

Ayer, A. J. "The Principle of Utility," in *Philosophical Essays*, London, 1954, pp. 250-270.

Bachrach, Peter. *The Theory of Democratic Elitism: A Critique*, Boston, 1967.

Bagehot, Walter. *The English Constitution*, ed. R.H.S. Crossman, London, 1963.

Barker, Anthony, and Michael Rush. *The Member of Parliament and His Information*, London, 1970.

Barker, Ernest. "Burke and His Bristol Constituency, 1774-1780," in *Essays on Government*, 2d ed., London, 1951, ch. VI.

Barry, Brian. *The Liberal Theory of Justice: A Critical Examination of the Principal Doctrines in* A Theory of Justice *by John Rawls*, Oxford, 1973.

————. *Political Argument*, London, 1965.

————, and Douglas W. Rae. "Political Evaluation," in Fred I. Greenstein and Nelson W. Polsby (eds.), *Handbook of Political Science*, vol. I, *Political Science: Scope and Theory*, Reading, Mass., 1975, pp. 337-401.

Batchelder, Alan B. *The Economics of Poverty*, 2d ed., New York, 1971.

Bay, Christian. "Politics and Pseudopolitics: A Critical Evaluation of Some Behavioral Literature," *American Political Science Review* 59 (March 1965), pp. 39-51.

Bealey, Frank, Jean Blondel, and W. P. McCann. *Constituency Politics: A Study of Newcastle-under-Lyme*, London, 1965.

Beer, Samuel H. *British Politics in the Collectivist Age*, New York, 1969.

Bell, Daniel. *The Coming of Post-Industrial Society: A Venture in Social Forecasting*, New York, 1973.

Bentham, Jeremy. "Anti-Senatica," *Smith College Studies in History* 11 (July 1926), pp. 209-267.

―――. *The Book of Fallacies*, in John Bowring (ed.), *The Works of Jeremy Bentham*, Edinburgh, 1843, vol. II, pp. 375-487.

―――. *Chrestomathia*, in *Works*, vol. VIII, pp. 1-191.

―――. *Constitutional Code*, in *Works*, vol. IX, pp. 1-662.

―――. *The Elements of the Art of Packing*, in *Works*, vol. V, pp. 61-186.

―――. *A Fragment on Government*, ed. Wilfred Harrison, Oxford, 1960.

―――. *An Introduction to the Principles of Morals and Legislation*, ed. J. H. Burns and H.L.A. Hart, London, 1970.

―――. *Leading Principles of a Constitutional Code, For Any State*, in *Works*, vol. II, pp. 267-274.

―――. *Plan of Parliamentary Reform*, in *Works*, vol. III, pp. 433-557.

―――. *Radical Reform Bill*, in *Works*, vol. III, pp. 558-597.

Bentley, Arthur F. *The Process of Government*, Bloomington, Ind., 1949.

Berelson, Bernard R., Paul F. Lazarsfeld, and William N. McPhee. *Voting: A Study of Opinion Formation in a Presidential Campaign*, Chicago, 1954.

Berg, Irwin A., and Bernard M. Bass (eds.). *Conformity and Deviation*, New York, 1961.

Berrington, Hugh. "Partisanship and Dissidence in the Nineteenth-Century House of Commons," *Parliamentary Affairs* 21 (Autumn 1968), pp. 338-374.

Birch, A. H. *Responsible and Representative Government*, London, 1964.

———. *Representation*, London, 1971.

Blackie, J. S. "Prussia and the Prussian System," *Westminster Review* 37 (January 1842), pp. 134-171.

Blau, Peter M. *The Dynamics of Bureaucracy: A Study of Interpersonal Relationships in Two Government Agencies*, rev. ed., Chicago, 1963.

———, and Otis Dudley Duncan. *The American Occupational Structure*, New York, 1967.

Blumberg, Paul. *Industrial Democracy: The Sociology of Participation*, London, 1968.

Bottomore, T. B. *Classes in Modern Society*, New York, 1966.

———. "The Class Structure in Western Europe," in Margaret Archer and Salvador Giner (eds.), *Contemporary Europe: Class, Status and Power*, London, 1971, pp. 388-407.

———. *Elites and Society*, London, 1964.

Bowles, Samuel, and Herbert Gintis. *Schooling in Capitalist America: Educational Reform and the Contradictions of Economic Life*, New York, 1976.

Bryce, James. *The American Commonwealth*, 2d ed., London, 1891.

Brzezinski, Zbigniew. *Between Two Ages: America's Role in the Technetronic Era*, New York, 1970.

Burke, Edmund. *Burke's Politics*, ed. Ross Hoffman and Paul Levack, New York, 1959.

Burnham, James. *The Managerial Revolution*, New York, 1942.

Burnham, Walter Dean. "The Changing Shape of the American Political Universe," *American Political Science Review* 59 (March 1965), pp. 7-28.

Butler, David E. *The Electoral System in Britain Since 1918*, 2d ed., Oxford, 1963.

———, and Anthony King. *The British General Election of 1964*, London, 1965.

———, and Richard Rose. *The British General Election of 1959*, London, 1960.

———, and Donald Stokes. *Political Change in Britain: The Evolution of Electoral Choice*, 2d ed., London, 1974.

Calvin, John. *Institutes of the Christian Religion*, tr. John Allen, Philadelphia, 1936.

Campbell, Angus, Philip E. Converse, Warren E. Miller, and Donald E. Stokes. *The American Voter*, New York, 1960.

Carlyle, Thomas. "The New Downing Street," *Works of Thomas Carlyle*, New York, 1898, vol. xx, pp. 127-171.

Central Statistical Office. *Annual Abstract of Statistics, 1975*, London, 1975.

Cole, G.D.H. *The Future of Local Government*, London, 1921.

Comte, Auguste. *Cours de philosophie positive*, Paris, 1877.

Connolly, William E. (ed.). *The Bias of Pluralism*, New York, 1969.

Converse, Philip E. "The Nature of Belief Systems in Mass Publics," in David E. Apter (ed.), *Ideology and Discontent*, New York, 1964.

Crozier, Michel. *The Bureaucratic Phenomenon*, Chicago, 1965.

Dahl, Robert A. *After the Revolution? Authority in a Good Society*, New Haven, 1970.

———. *Democracy in the United States: Promise and Performance*, Chicago, 1972.

———. *Polyarchy: Participation and Opposition*, New Haven, 1971.

Dahl, Robert A. *A Preface to Democratic Theory*, Chicago, 1956.

——. *Who Governs? Democracy and Power in an American City*, New Haven, 1961.

——, and Edward R. Tufte. *Size and Democracy*, Stanford, 1973.

Dahrendorf, Ralf. "Democracy Without Liberty: An Essay on the Politics of the Other-Directed Man," in Seymour M. Lipset and Leo Lowenthal (eds.), *Culture and Social Character: The Work of David Riesman Reviewed*, New York, 1961, pp. 175-206.

——. "Recent Changes in the Class Structure of European Societies," *Daedalus* 93 (Winter 1964), pp. 225-270.

Davis, Lane. "The Cost of Realism: Contemporary Restatements of Democracy," *Western Political Quarterly* 17 (March 1964), pp. 37-46.

Deane, Philip, and W. A. Cole. *British Economic Growth, 1688-1959: Trends and Structure*, Cambridge, England, 1964.

Dodd, Lawrence. *Coalitions in Parliamentary Government*, Princeton, 1976.

Dogan, Mattei. "Political Ascent in a Class Society: French Deputies, 1870-1958," in Dwaine Marvick (ed.), *Political Decision-Makers*, Glencoe, Ill., 1961.

Dray, William H. *Philosophy of History*, Englewood Cliffs, N.J., 1964.

Droop, Henry R. "On the Political and Social Effects of Different Methods of Electing Representatives," *Papers Read Before the Juridical Society, 1863-70*, London, 1871, vol. III, pp. 469-507.

Duijker, H.C.J., and N. H. Frijda. *National Character and National Stereotypes*, Amsterdam, 1960.

Duncan, Graeme, and Steven Lukes. "The New Democracy," *Political Studies* 11 (June 1963), pp. 156-177.

Duverger, Maurice. *Political Parties, Their Organization and Activity in the Modern State*, tr. Barbara and Robert North, New York, 1963.

Eckstein, Harry. *A Theory of Stable Democracy*, Princeton, 1961.

Euben, J. Peter. "Political Science and Political Silence," in Philip Green and Sanford Levinson (eds.), *Power and Community: Dissenting Essays in Political Science*, New York, 1969, pp. 3-58.

Eulau, Heinz. "Changing Views of Representation," in *Micro-Macro Political Analysis: Accents of Inquiry*, Chicago, 1969, pp. 76-102.

————, and Kenneth Prewitt. *Labyrinths of Democracy: Adaptations, Linkages, Representation and Policies in Urban Politics*, Indianapolis, 1973.

Farkas, Joseph. "One Man, ¼ Vote," *New York Times* (March 29, 1974), p. 22.

Fawcett, Millicent G. "Proportional Representation and Hare's Scheme Explained," in Henry Fawcett and Millicent Fawcett, *Essays and Lectures on Social and Political Subjects*, London, 1872, pp. 336-368.

The Federalist Papers, ed. Clinton Rossiter, New York, 1961.

Flathman, Richard E. *The Public Interest: An Essay Concerning the Normative Discourse of Politics*, New York, 1966.

Frederickson, George (ed.). *Neighborhood Control in the 1970's: Politics, Administration and Citizen Participation*, New York, 1973.

Friend, J. K., and W. N. Jessop. *Local Government and*

Strategic Choice: An Operational Research Approach to the Process of Public Planning, London, 1969.

Fry, Brian R., and Richard F. Winters. "The Politics of Redistribution," *American Political Science Review* 64 (June 1970), pp. 508-522.

Gash, Norman. *Politics in the Age of Peel: A Study in the Techniques of Parliamentary Representation, 1830-50*, London, 1953.

Giddens, Anthony. *The Class Structure of the Advanced Societies*, London, 1973.

Goldthorpe, John H., David Lockwood, Frank Bechhofer, and Jennifer Platt. *The Affluent Worker in the Class Structure*, Cambridge, England, 1969.

Gouldner, Alvin W. "Metaphysical Pathos and the Theory of Bureaucracy," *American Political Science Review* 49 (June 1955), pp. 496-507.

———. *Patterns of Industrial Bureaucracy: A Case Study of Modern Factory Administration*, Glencoe, Ill., 1955.

Greenstein, Fred. "New Light on Changing American Values: A Forgotten Body of Survey Data," *Social Forces* 42 (May 1964), pp. 441-450.

Griffith, J.A.G. *Central Departments and Local Authorities*, Toronto, 1965.

Guttsman, W. L. "The British Political Elite and Class Structure," in Philip Stanworth and Anthony Giddens (eds.), *Elites and Power in British Society*, Cambridge, England, 1974.

Hanham, Harold J. *Elections and Party Management: Politics in the Time of Disraeli and Gladstone*, London, 1959.

Hare, Thomas. *The Election of Representatives: Parliamentary and Municipal*, 3d ed., London, 1865.

Heckhausen, Heinz. *The Anatomy of Achievement Motivation*, New York, 1967.

Hermens, Ferdinand A. *Democracy or Anarchy? A Study of Proportional Representation*, South Bend, Ind., 1941

Hill, Dilys M. *Participating in Local Affairs*, Harmondsworth, 1970.

Hoffmann, Stanley (ed.). *In Search of France*, Cambridge, Mass., 1963.

Hume, David. *A Treatise of Human Nature*, ed. L. A. Selby-Bigge, Oxford, 1960.

————. "Of the Independency of Parliament," *Essays: Moral, Political and Literary*, Oxford, 1963.

Humes, Samuel, and Eileen M. Martin. *The Structure of Local Government Throughout the World*, The Hague, 1961.

Huntington, Samuel P. *Political Order in Changing Societies*, New Haven, 1968.

————. "Postindustrial Politics: How Benign Will it Be?" *Comparative Politics* 6 (January 1974), pp. 163-191.

Inglehart, Ronald. *The Silent Revolution: Political Change Among Western Publics*, Princeton, 1976.

Inkeles, Alex, and Daniel J. Levinson. "National Character: The Study of Modal Personality and Socio-Cultural Systems," in Gardner Lindzey and Elliot Aronson (eds.), *The Handbook of Social Psychology*, 2d ed., Reading, Mass., 1969, vol. IV, pp. 418-506.

Inter-Parliamentary Union. *Parliaments: A Comparative Study on the Structure and Functioning of Representative Institutions in Fifty-Five Countries*, rev. ed., prepared by Michel Ameller, London, 1966.

Jackman, Robert W. *Politics and Social Equality: A Comparative Analysis*, New York, 1975.

Jones, Charles O. "Representation in Congress," *American Political Science Review* 55 (December 1961), pp. 358-367.

Jouvenal, Bertrand de. "Rousseau, The Pessimistic Evolutionist," *Yale French Studies* 28 (1961-62), pp. 83-96.

Kariel, Henry. *The Decline of American Pluralism*, Stanford, 1961.

———— (ed.). *Frontiers of Democratic Theory*, New York, 1970.

Katz, Alihu, and Brenda Danet (eds.). *Bureaucracy and the Public*, New York, 1973.

Kelley, Stanley, Jr. "Campaign Debates: Some Facts and Issues," *Public Opinion Quarterly* 26 (Fall 1962), pp. 351-366.

————, Richard E. Ayres, and William G. Bowen. "Registration and Voting: Putting First Things First," *American Political Science Review* 61 (June 1967), pp. 359-377.

Key, V. O. *Public Opinion and American Democracy*, New York, 1961.

Kluckhohn, Clyde. "Have There Been Any Discernible Shifts in American Values During the Past Generation?" in Elting E. Morison (ed.), *The American Style*, New York, 1958, pp. 145-217.

Kuznets, Simon. "Income Distribution and Changes in Consumption," in Hoke S. Simpson (ed.), *The Changing American Population*, New York, 1962, pp. 21-58.

Lakeman, Enid. *How Democracies Vote: A Study of Majority and Proportional Electoral Systems*, 3d ed., London, 1970.

Lane, Robert E. *Political Ideology: Why the American Common Man Believes What He Does*, New York, 1962.

————, and David O. Sears. *Public Opinion*, Englewood Cliffs, N.J., 1964.

Lang, Andrew. *Life, Letters and Diaries of Sir Stafford Northcote*, vol. II, Edinburgh, 1890.

Laski, Harold J. *The Limitations of the Expert*, London, 1931.

"Learning from Error," *New York Times* (August 12, 1972), p. 22.

Lebergott, Stanley. *Wealth and Want*, Princeton, 1976.

Lindsay, A. D. *The Modern Democratic State*, New York, 1962.

Lipset, Seymour Martin. *The First New Nation: The United States in Historical and Comparative Perspective*, New York, 1963.

————. *Political Man: The Social Bases of Politics*, New York, 1963.

————, and Reinhard Bendix. *Social Mobility in Industrial Society: A Study of Political Sociology*, Berkeley, 1959.

————, and Leo Lowenthal (eds.). *Culture and Social Character: The Work of David Riesman Reviewed*, New York, 1961.

Littlejohn, James. *Social Stratification*, London, 1972.

Lowell, A. Lawrence. *The Government of England*, New York, 1908.

Macaulay, T. B. "[James] Mill on Government," in *Miscellaneous Writings of Lord Macaulay*, London, 1860, vol. I, pp. 282-322.

————. *Speeches and Poems*, New York, 1867.

MacDonald, Henry M. (ed.). *The Intellectual in Politics*, Austin, Texas, 1966.

Mackenzie, W.J.M. *Free Elections*, New York, 1958.

Mackintosh, James. "Universal Suffrage," *Edinburgh Review* 31 (December 1818), pp. 165-203.

Mackintosh, John P. *The British Cabinet*, London, 1962.

―――. *The Devolution of Power: Local Democracy, Regionalism and Nationalism*, Harmondsworth, 1968.

―――. "Reform of the Commons: The Case for Specialized Committees," in Gerhard Loewenberg (ed.), *Modern Parliaments: Change or Decline?*, Chicago, 1971.

Mannheim, Karl. *Ideology and Utopia*, tr. Louis Wirth and Edward Shils, London, 1963.

Marshall, T. H. *Class, Citizenship, and Social Development*, New York, 1964.

―――. *Social Policy in the 20th Century*, 3d ed., London, 1970.

Martindale, Don (ed.). *National Character in the Perspective of the Social Sciences*, The Annals 370 (March 1967).

Martineau, Harriet. *Society in America*, New York, 1837.

Marx, Karl. *A Contribution to the Critique of Political Economy*, ed. Maurice Dobb, tr. S. W. Ryazanskaya, New York, 1970.

―――, and Frederick Engels. *The German Ideology*, ed. R. Pascal, New York, 1947.

―――, and Frederick Engels. *The Holy Family*, tr. R. Dixon, Moscow, 1956.

McClelland, David C. *The Achieving Society*, New York, 1961.

McClosky, Herbert. "Consensus and Ideology in American Politics," *American Political Science Review* 58 (June 1964), pp. 361-382.

McKenzie, Robert T. *British Political Parties: The Distribution of Power Within the Conservative and Labour Parties,* 2d ed., New York, 1964.

———, and Allan Silver. *Angels in Marble: Working Class Conservatives in Urban England,* Chicago, 1968.

Meadows, Dennis L., Donella H. Meadows, Jorgen Randers, and William W. Behrens III. *The Limits of Growth,* A Report for the Club of Rome, New York, 1972.

Medawar, P. B. *The Art of the Soluble,* London, 1967.

Mencher, Samuel. *Poor Law to Poverty Program: Economic Security Policy in Britain and the United States,* Pittsburgh, 1967.

Merriam, Charles. *The New Democracy and the New Despotism,* New York, 1939.

Merton, Robert K. "Bureaucratic Structure and Personality," *Social Forces* 18 (May 1940), pp. 560-568.

Mesick, Jane L. *The English Traveller in America, 1785-1835,* New York, 1922.

Milbrath, Lester. *Political Participation: How and Why Do People Get Involved in Politics?* Chicago, 1965.

Mill, James. "The Ballot," *Westminster Review* 13 (July 1830), pp. 1-39.

———. "Education," in W. H. Burston (ed.), *James Mill on Education,* Cambridge, England, 1969, pp. 41-119.

———. *An Essay on Government,* Indianapolis, 1955.

———. *Fragment on Mackintosh,* London, 1870.

Miller, Warren E., and Donald E. Stokes. "Constituency Influence in Congress," *American Political Science Review* 57 (March 1963), pp. 45-56.

Mosca, Gaetano. *Teorica dei governi e governo parlamentare,* 2d ed., Turin, 1925.

Neubauer, Deane E. "Some Conditions of Democracy," *American Political Science Review* 61 (December 1967), pp. 1002-1009.

Nie, Norman H. "Mass Belief Systems Revisited: Political Change and Attitude Structure," *Journal of Politics* 36 (August 1974), pp. 540-591.

Niskanen, William A., Jr. *Bureaucracy and Representative Government*, Chicago, 1971.

Nordlinger, Eric A. *The Working-Class Tories: Authority, Deference and Stable Democracy*, Berkeley and Los Angeles, 1967.

Oakeshott, Michael. *Rationalism in Politics, and Other Essays*, London, 1962.

Olson, Mancur, and Hans H. Landsberg (eds.), *The No-Growth Society*, New York, 1973.

Ostrogorski, Moisei. *Democracy and the Organization of Political Parties*, New York, 1964.

Parry, Geraint. *Political Elites*, New York, 1969.

Partridge, P. H. *Consent and Consensus*, London, 1971.

Pateman, Carole. *Participation and Democratic Theory*, Cambridge, England, 1970.

Peacock, Alan T., and Jack Wiseman. *The Growth of Public Expenditure in the United Kingdom*, Princeton, 1961.

Pennock, J. Roland. "Democracy and Leadership," in William N. Chambers and Robert H. Salisbury (eds.), *Democracy Today: Problems and Prospects*, New York, 1962, pp. 122-158.

Pitkin, Hanna Fenichel. *The Concept of Representation*, Berkeley and Los Angeles, 1967.

Plamenatz, John. *Democracy and Illusion: An Examination of Certain Aspects of Modern Democratic Theory*, London, 1973.

————. "Electoral Studies and Democratic Theory: A

British View," *Political Studies* 6 (February 1958), pp. 1-9.

Plato. *Republic*, tr. Paul Shorey, Cambridge, Mass., 1963.

Political and Economic Planning. *Reforming the Commons*, vol. 31, London, 1965.

Pollard, Sidney, and David W. Crossley. *The Wealth of Britain, 1085-1966*, London, 1968.

Polsby, Nelson W. *Community Power and Political Theory*, New Haven, 1963.

Popper, Karl. *The Poverty of Historicism*, New York, 1960.

Presthus, Robert. *The Organizational Society: An Analysis and a Theory*, New York, 1962.

Pulzer, Peter G. J. *Political Representation and Elections in Britain*, rev. ed., London, 1972.

Putnam, Robert D. *The Beliefs of Politicians: Ideology, Conflict and Democracy in Britain and Italy*, New Haven, 1973.

Rae, Douglas W. *The Political Consequences of Electoral Laws*, New Haven, 1967.

Ranney, Austin. *Pathways to Parliament: Candidate Selection in Britain*, Madison, Wis., 1965.

————, and Willmoore Kendall. *Democracy and the American Party System*, New York, 1956.

Rawls, John. *A Theory of Justice*, Cambridge, Mass., 1971.

Redlich, Josef, and Francis W. Hirst. *The History of Local Government in England*, 2d ed., introduction by Bryan Keith-Lucas, London, 1970 (originally Part I of *Local Government in England*, London, 1903).

Rees, Ioan Bowen. *Government by Community*, London, 1971.

Reissman, Leonard. *Inequality in American Society: Social Stratification*, Glenview, Ill., 1973.

Rejai, Mostafa (ed.). *Decline of Ideology?*, Chicago, 1971.

Rest, James R. "The Hierarchical Nature of Moral Judgment: A Study of Patterns of Comprehension and Preference of Moral Stages," in James R. Rest, Lawrence Kohlberg, and Elliot Turiel (eds.), *Recent Research in Moral Development*, forthcoming.

————, Elliot Turiel, and Lawrence Kohlberg. "Level of Moral Development as a Determinant of Preference and Comprehension of the Moral Judgments Made by Others," *Journal of Personality* 37 (June 1969), pp. 225-252.

Richardson, Benjamin Ward. *The Health of Nations: A Review of the Works of Edwin Chadwick*, London, 1887, reprinted 1965.

Rieff, Philip (ed.). *On Intellectuals: Theoretical Studies, Case Studies*, New York, 1969.

Riesman, David. *The Lonely Crowd: A Study of the Changing American Character*, New Haven, 1950.

Robson, W. A. *Local Government in Crisis*, London, 1966.

Rokkan, Stein. *Citizens, Elections, Parties: Approaches to the Comparative Study of the Processes of Development*, New York, 1970.

Rose, Richard. "Class and Party Divisions: Britain as a Test Case," *Sociology* 2 (May 1968), pp. 129-162.

————. "England: A Traditionally Modern Political Culture," in Lucian W. Pye and Sidney Verba (eds.). *Political Culture and Political Development*, Princeton, 1965, pp. 83-129.

224

————. *Influencing Voters: A Study of Campaign Rationality*, New York, 1967.

Ross, J.F.S. *The Irish Election System*, London, 1959.

Rousseas, Stephen W., and James Farganis. "American Politics and the End of Ideology," *British Journal of Sociology* 14 (December 1963), pp. 347-362.

Rousseau, Jean-Jacques. *Considérations sur le gouvernement de Pologne*, in C. E. Vaughan (ed.), *The Political Writings of Jean-Jacques Rousseau*, Oxford, 1962, vol. II, pp. 424-516.

————. *Discours. Si le rétablissement des sciences et des arts à contribué à épurer les moeurs*, in *Oeuvres complètes*, Paris, 1905, vol. I, pp. 1-20.

————. *Discours sur l'origine et les fondements de l'inégalité parmi les hommes*, in *Political Writings*, vol. I, pp. 125-220.

————. *Du contrat social*, in *Political Writings*, vol. II, pp. 21-134.

————. *Économie politique*, in *Political Writings*, vol. I, pp. 237-280.

————. *Émile*, tr. Barbara Foxley, London, 1948.

————. *Politics and the Arts: Letter to M. d'Alembert on the Theatre*, tr. Allan Bloom, Glencoe, Ill., 1960.

————. *"Préface" à Narcisse*, in *Oeuvres complètes*, Paris, 1959, vol. II, pp. 959-974.

————. *Projet de constitution pour la Corse*, in *Political Writings*, vol. II, pp. 306-356.

Royal Commission on Local Government in England. *Report*, vol. I, Cmnd. 4040, London, 1969.

Runciman, W. G. *Relative Deprivation and Social Justice: A Study of Attitudes to Social Inequality in Twentieth-Century England*, London, 1966.

Rush, Michael. *The Selection of Parliamentary Candidates*, London, 1969.

Russett, Bruce M. *Trends in World Politics*, New York, 1965.

Sabine, George. *A History of Political Theory*, 3d ed., New York, 1961.

Sadek, S.E.M. *The Balance Point Between Local Autonomy and National Control*, The Hague, 1972.

Sartori, Giovanni. *Democratic Theory*, New York, 1965.

Schiller, Bradley. *The Economics of Poverty and Discrimination*, Englewood Cliffs, N.J., 1973.

Schumpeter, Joseph. *Capitalism, Socialism and Democracy*, 3d ed., New York, 1962.

Sears, David O., and Jonathan L. Freedman. "Selective Exposure to Information: A Critical View," *Public Opinion Quarterly* 31 (Summer 1967), pp. 194-213.

Selznick, Philip. *TVA and the Grass Roots*, New York, 1966.

Serrentino, Constance. "Comparing Employment Shifts in 10 Industrialized Countries," *Monthly Labor Review* 94 (October 1971), pp. 3-11.

Sharpe, L. J. "Elected Representatives in Local Government," *British Journal of Sociology* 13 (September 1962), pp. 189-209.

———. *Why Local Democracy*, Fabian Tract 361, London, 1965.

Shils, Edward. *The Intellectuals and the Powers and Other Essays*, Chicago, 1972.

Shklar, Judith N. *Men and Citizens: A Study of Rousseau's Social Theory*, Cambridge, England, 1969.

Skinner, Quentin. "The Empirical Theorists of Democracy and Their Critics: A Plague on Both Their Houses," *Political Theory* 1 (August 1973), pp. 287-306.

Spitz, David. *Democracy and the Challenge of Power*, New York, 1958.

Taylor, Charles. "Neutrality in Political Science," in Peter Laslett and W. G. Runciman (eds.), *Philosophy, Politics and Society*, 3d series, New York, 1967, pp. 25-57.

Thompson, Dennis F. *The Democratic Citizen: Social Science and Democratic Theory in the 20th Century*, Cambridge, England, 1970.

Titmuss, Richard M. *Income Distribution and Social Change: A Study in Criticism*, London, 1962.

Tocqueville, Alexis de. *De la démocratie en Amérique*, Paris, 1951.

Trenaman, Joseph, and Denis McQuail. *Television and the Political Image: A Study of the Impact of Television on the 1959 General Election*, London, 1961.

Truman, David. *The Governmental Process: Political Interests and Public Opinion*, New York, 1951.

Unkelbach, Helmut. *Grundlägen der Wahlsystematik; Stabilitätsbedingungen der parliamentarischen Demokratie*, Göttingen, 1956.

Verba, Sidney, and Norman H. Nie. *Participation in America: Political Democracy and Social Equality*, New York, 1972.

Vernon, M. D. *Human Motivation*, Cambridge, England, 1969.

Vile, M.J.C. *Constitutionalism and the Separation of Powers*, Oxford, 1967.

Walker, Jack L. "A Critique of the Elitist Theory of Democracy," *American Political Science Review* 60 (June 1966), pp. 285-295.

Walkland, S. A. *The Legislative Process in Great Britain*, London, 1968.

Webb, Sidney, and Beatrice Webb. *English Poor Law History: Part II: The Last Hundred Years*, London, 1929.

Weber, Max. "Class, Status, Party," in *From Max Weber*, tr. and ed. H. H. Gerth and C. Wright Mills, New York, 1946, pp. 180-195.

―――. *The Protestant Ethic and the Spirit of Capitalism*, tr. Talcott Parsons, New York, 1958.

―――. *The Theory of Social and Economic Organization*, tr. A. M. Henderson and Talcott Parsons, Glencoe, Ill., 1947.

―――. *Wirtschaft und Gesellschaft*, Tübingen, 1956.

Wheare, K. C. *Legislatures*, London, 1963.

White, Winston. *Beyond Conformity*, New York, 1961.

Wickwar, William Hardy. *The Political Theory of Local Government*, Columbia, S.C., 1970.

Wilson, James Q., and Edward Banfield. "Public-Regardingness as a Value Premise in Voting Behavior," *American Political Science Review* 58 (December 1964), pp. 876-887.

Wolff, Robert Paul. *The Poverty of Liberalism*, Boston, 1968.

Wolfinger, Raymond E., and John Osgood Field. "Political Ethos and the Structure of City Government," *American Political Science Review* 60 (June 1966), pp. 306-326.

Yates, Douglas T. *Neighborhood Democracy: The Politics and Impacts of Decentralization*, Lexington, Mass., 1973.

Index

achievement ethic, 30-37, 163, 165, 189
Adams, John C., 94n, 123n
Adelman, Irma, 27n
Agger, Robert E., 42n
Albrow, Martin, 65n, 66n
Alford, Robert, 126n, 170n
Almond, Gabriel, 39n, 42, 147n
American society, 34, 38-39, 72, 74, 75, 160
Anderson, Charles, 167n
Andreano, Ralph, 27n
Annan, Noel, 6n, 108n
Anschutz, R. P., 6n, 8, 19n, 57n, 108n
Anti-Corn Law movement, 52
apathy, 53, 144-45, 166, 194
Apter, David E., 77n
Archer, Margaret, 168n
aristocracy, 37, 48, 64, 68, 79, 93, 94, 115
Aristotle, 20n, 93, 95, 96, 176
Aron, Raymond, 88n, 167n
Aronson, Elliot, 32n
Asch, Solomon E., 75n
Athens, ancient, 38-39, 81, 122
Atkinson, John W., 34n
Austria, 22
authoritarianism, 143
Ayer, A. J., 15n
Ayres, Richard E., 23n

Bachrach, Peter, 8n, 51n, 192n, 193n, 195n
Bagehot, Walter, 82-83, 86, 92, 93n, 110n, 178n, 185
Banfield, Edward, 40n

Barker, Anthony, 118n
Barker, Ernest, 116n, 122n
Barry, Brian, 15n, 101n, 199n
Bass, Bernard M., 75n
Batchelder, Alan B., 168n
Bay, Christian, 139n, 193n, 195n
Bealey, Frank, 40n
Bechhofer, Frank, 170n
Beer, Samuel, 116n, 118n, 119n, 120n
Behrens, William W., 169n
Bell, Daniel, 165n
Bendix, Reinhard, 168n
Bentham, Jeremy: on annual elections, 114; boards and committees, 66-67; customs, 161; decentralization, 131; education, 29; higher pleasures, 56, 108n; interests, 14, 25, 68; leadership, 7, 9, 91; Legislative Commission, 122n; mixed government, 94; as a "one-eyed" theorist, 178; U.S. Senate, 95n
Bentley, Arthur F., 193n
Berelson, Bernard, 192n
Berg, Irwin A., 75n
Berrington, Hugh, 119n
Birch, A. H., 109n, 120n
Blackie, J. S., 66n
Blau, Peter M., 168n
Blondel, Jean, 40n
Bloom, Allan, 45n
Blumberg, Paul, 43n
Board of Guardians, 128
Bottomore, T. B., 88, 168n, 170n, 193n, 195n
Bowen, William G., 23n

229

Library of Congress Cataloging in Publication Data

Thompson, Dennis Frank.
    John Stuart Mill and representative government.

    Bibliography: p.
    Includes index.
    1. Mill, John Stuart, 1806-1873—Political science.
2. Mill, John Stuart, 1806-1873. Considerations on Representative Government. 3. Representative government and representation. I. Title.
JC223.M66T48   321.8   76-3023
ISBN 0-691-07582-4